Ethnic Celebrations Around the World

Written and illustrated by Nancy Everix

Cover by Vanessa Filkins

Copyright © Good Apple, 1991

Good Apple
1204 Buchanan St., Box 299
Carthage, IL 62321-0299

SIMON & SCHUSTER *A Paramount Communications Company*

Copyright © Good Apple, 1991

ISBN No. 0-86653-607-8

Printing No. 987

Good Apple
1204 Buchanan St., Box 299
Carthage, IL 62321-0299

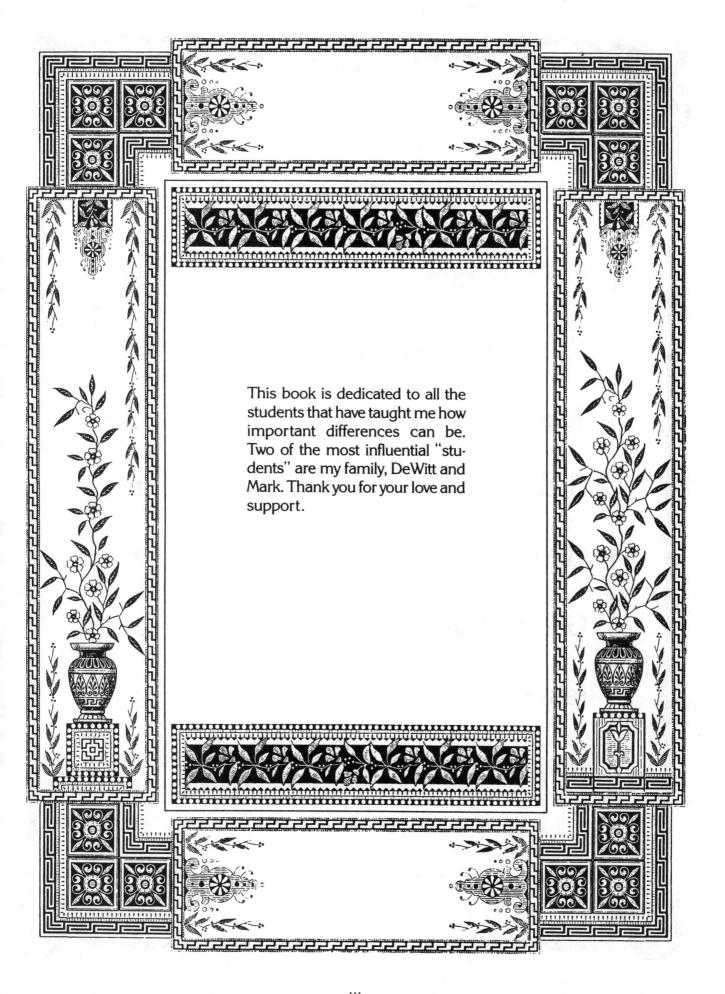

This book is dedicated to all the students that have taught me how important differences can be. Two of the most influential "students" are my family, DeWitt and Mark. Thank you for your love and support.

GA1326

Table of Contents

GA1326

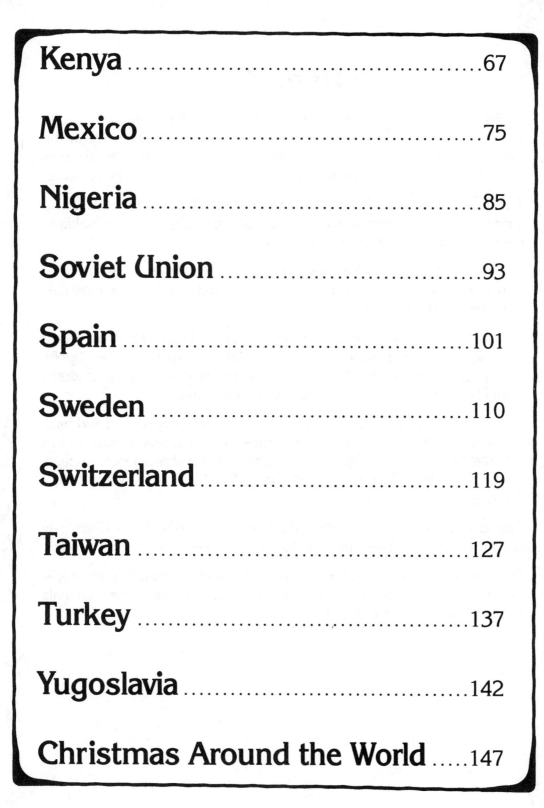

GA1326

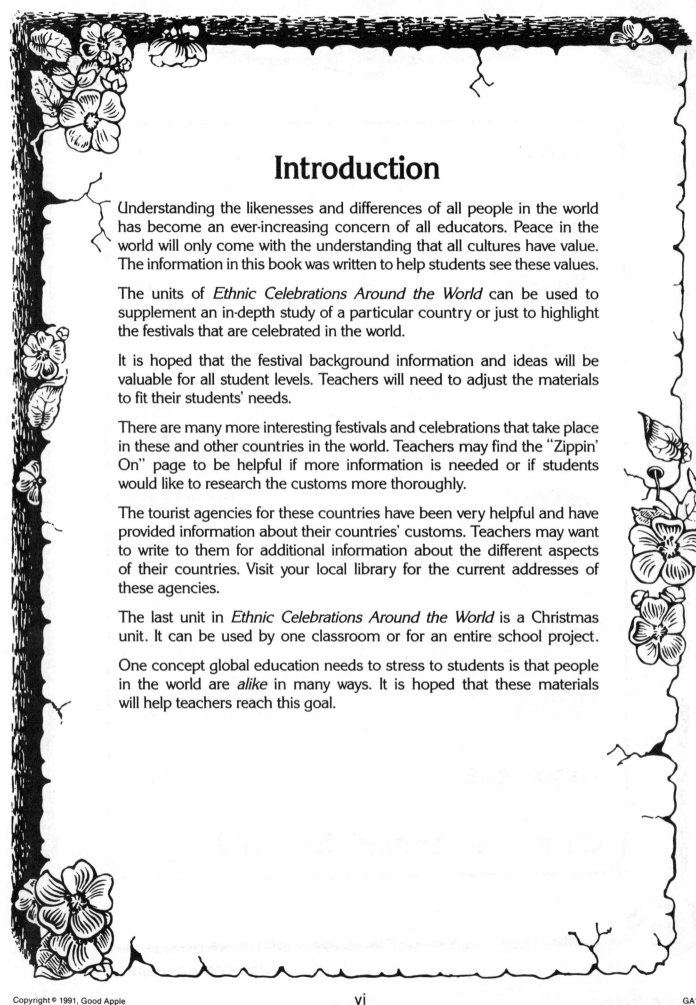

Introduction

Understanding the likenesses and differences of all people in the world has become an ever-increasing concern of all educators. Peace in the world will only come with the understanding that all cultures have value. The information in this book was written to help students see these values.

The units of *Ethnic Celebrations Around the World* can be used to supplement an in-depth study of a particular country or just to highlight the festivals that are celebrated in the world.

It is hoped that the festival background information and ideas will be valuable for all student levels. Teachers will need to adjust the materials to fit their students' needs.

There are many more interesting festivals and celebrations that take place in these and other countries in the world. Teachers may find the "Zippin' On" page to be helpful if more information is needed or if students would like to research the customs more thoroughly.

The tourist agencies for these countries have been very helpful and have provided information about their countries' customs. Teachers may want to write to them for additional information about the different aspects of their countries. Visit your local library for the current addresses of these agencies.

The last unit in *Ethnic Celebrations Around the World* is a Christmas unit. It can be used by one classroom or for an entire school project.

One concept global education needs to stress to students is that people in the world are *alike* in many ways. It is hoped that these materials will help teachers reach this goal.

Research Notes
Page 1

Country's Official Name
Flag

Map
Population

Language

Physical Features

GA1326

Research Notes
Page 2

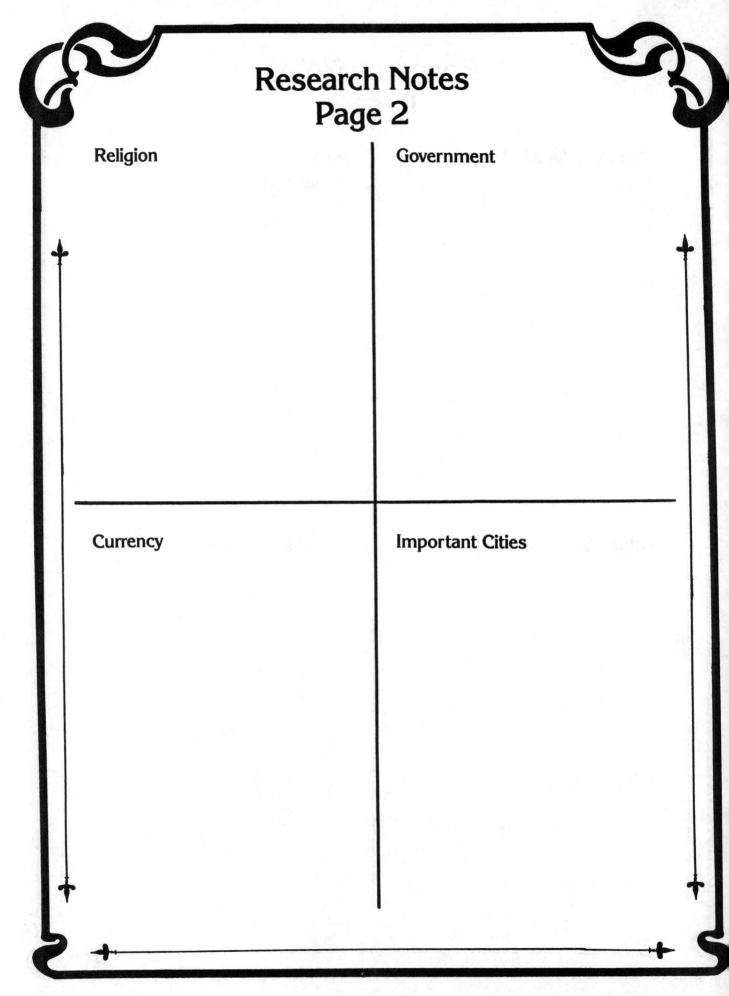

Religion

Government

Currency

Important Cities

2

GA1326

Research Notes
Page 3

National Holidays

Minerals

Agricultural Products

Exports

GA1326

Research Notes
Page 4

Imports

Industrial Products

Important People

Important Places

4

Research Notes
Page 5

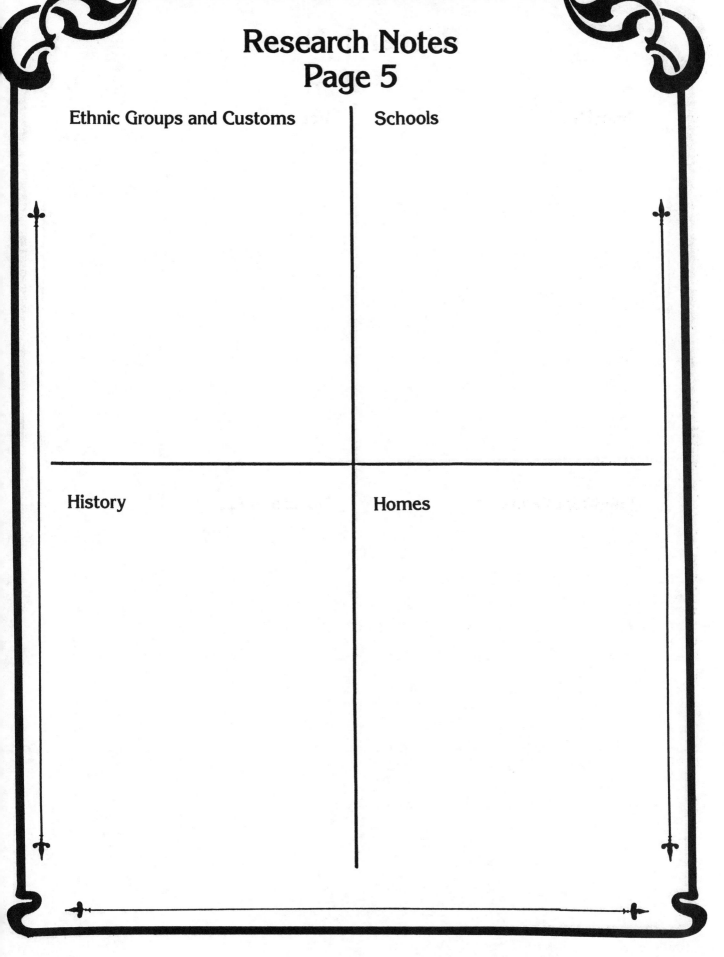

Ethnic Groups and Customs

Schools

History

Homes

GA1326

Research Notes
Page 6

Sports

Recreation

Foods

Music and Art

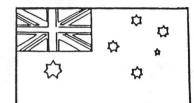 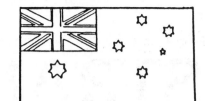 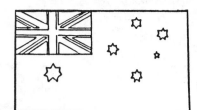

AUSTRALIA

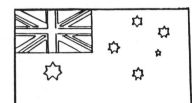  

GA1326

AUSTRALIA

1. Western Australia
2. Northern Territory
3. Queensland
4. South Australia
5. New South Wales
6. Victoria
7. Tasmania
8. Indian Ocean
9. Pacific Ocean

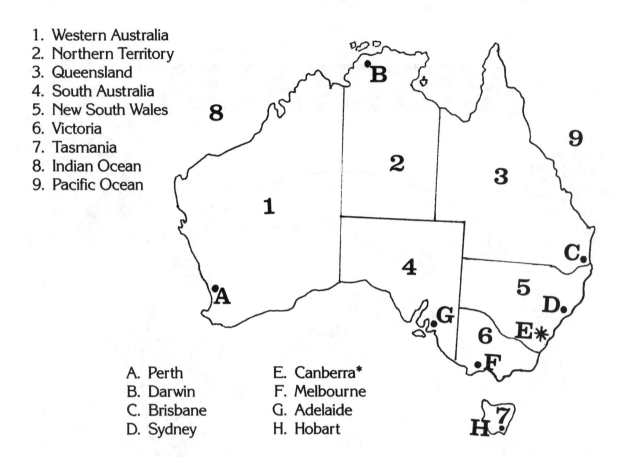

A. Perth
B. Darwin
C. Brisbane
D. Sydney

E. Canberra*
F. Melbourne
G. Adelaide
H. Hobart

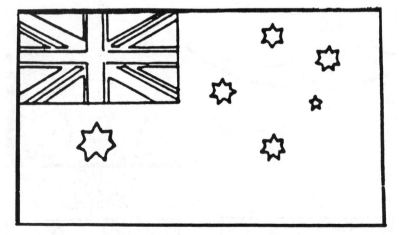

The basic design of Australia's flag came from the British Blue Ensign. The five stars of the Southern Cross constellation are to the right in the blue field. The larger star, known as the "Commonwealth Star" is below the upper-left corner. The seven points on the stars represent Australia's six states and one territory. This has been the official flag of Australia since 1909.

GA1326

AUSTRALIA DAY

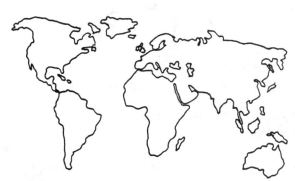

Australia Day is celebrated between January 26 and February 1. It marks the day the first white settlers arrived in Australia in 1788. Commemoration of the historical significance of the day seems to be lost in the social events taking place with families and good friends. These events include watching a cricket game, eating a good meal and having a good time together.

Research more about the first settlers. Is it true that they came from the prisons of England?

Locate the countries on the map that show where many settlers did come from.

ANZAC DAY

ANZAC Day is celebrated nationwide on April 25. ANZAC stands for the Australia, New Zealand Army Corps that fought in World War I. April 25 marks the day on which the combined army corps landed at Gallipoli in 1915.

Veterans pray together at dawn at the Shrine of Remembrance. This shrine was built so that on the eleventh hour of the eleventh month the sun strikes the word *love* in the inscription, "Greater *love* hath no man."

This phrase is part of a famous quotation. Try to find the whole quote and tell who said it.

Why was it used on this monument?

Research more about Australia's part in World War I, World War II and the Vietnam War.

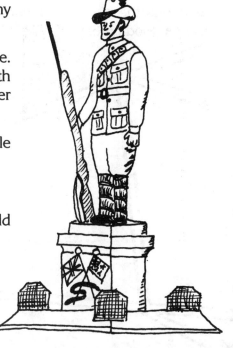

GA1326

MELBOURNE CUP

The Melbourne Cup takes place the first Tuesday in November. Approximately 80,000 or more people flood the Flemington Race Course. The Melbourne Cup is considered the country's most prestigious horse race.

This race began in 1861. It is a two-mile (3.22 km) race which brings the nation to a halt. The High Court closes, Parliament stops and the nation watches on television or listens on the radio.

Both men and women attend the race. Both are smartly dressed in suits, dresses and hats, all very fashionable.

Find out more about the winning horses, the life of a jockey or the gambling that takes place.

Design a hat appropriate for a man or woman to wear to the Melbourne Cup.

FOOTBALL
Australian Style

Football is the favorite sport of spectators in Australia. There are four kinds of football played, but the most popular is the eighteen-a-side Australian rules football. The Grand Final is an event that brings the city of Melbourne to a halt with 100,000 spectators engaged in the pursuit of having a good time.

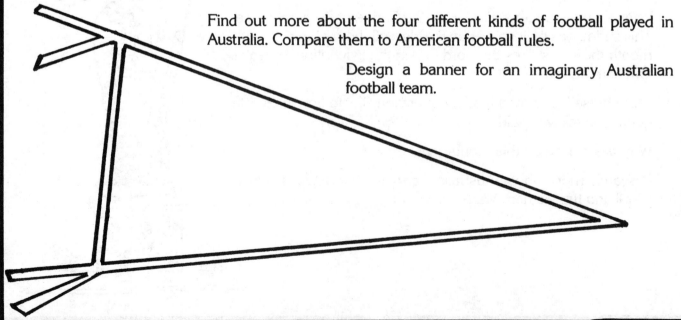

Find out more about the four different kinds of football played in Australia. Compare them to American football rules.

Design a banner for an imaginary Australian football team.

10

Adelaide Arts Festival

EXAMPLE:

3 _____
9 _____
▶4 _____
—
7 _____
8 _____
▶5 _____
—
2 _____

Adelaide, the capital of South Australia, also hosts the internationally known Arts Festival. It is held every other year. Leaders in music, drama and dance from many parts of the world join together in Australia for the cultural events. These events range from jazz to ballet and poetry readings to art exhibits.

Write a short poem about Australia using your phone number as the suggested number of syllables per line. Use the example at the top of this paper.

Could you or someone else in your class write a melody to go with it?

GRAND PRIX
Formula One Racing

Adelaide sparkles with excitement as it prepares for the annual motor racing event, the Grand Prix Formula One Race. It is one of the most popular races in the world and international teams arrive early to prepare for the event.

The race is held in late October or early November. The streets of the city of Adelaide are barricaded and the crowds line the raceway.

Two Australian folk heroes have emerged from this fast, flashy sport. They are Jack Brabham and Alan Jones.

Find out more about the Formula One race cars. Design one that your school could sponsor.

Who are some American drivers that might go to Australia for this race?

What kind of transportation problems might international racers face as they prepare to go to Adelaide?

Racing on city streets is considerably different from a racetrack. How do drivers prepare for this event?

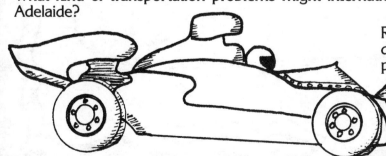

SYDNEY SURF CARNIVAL

The Sydney Surf Carnival opens with a huge parade. Two hundred thirty-six lifesaving clubs carry their clubs' colorful banners. The surf lifesaving clubs are groups of volunteer lifeguards that help swimmers and surfers in distress.

There is a series of colorful weekend carnivals around the coast which attracts large crowds.

Events that take place during the Carnival show split-second teamwork. There are staged rescue and resuscitation exercises. The teams are judged on their speed and execution.

The high point for spectators is the surfboat races. Crews in rowing boats compete along a buoy-marked course.

Read more about lifesaving. Try designing a surfboard.

Set up teams and each team makes a small boat. Race the team boats in an inflatable child's swimming pool.

GA1326

FAIRY PENGUIN PARADE

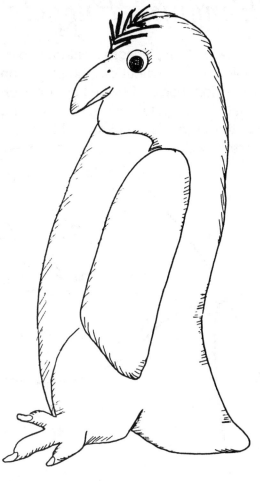

Near Melbourne, on Phillip Island, twilight arrives and so do the fairy penguins. Hundreds of tiny penguins waddle ashore and parade for the onlookers.

Research different kinds of penguins. List the names of the penguins. Draw a picture of each kind of penguin and make a list of the characteristics. You may need more room for your information. Use the back of this sheet.

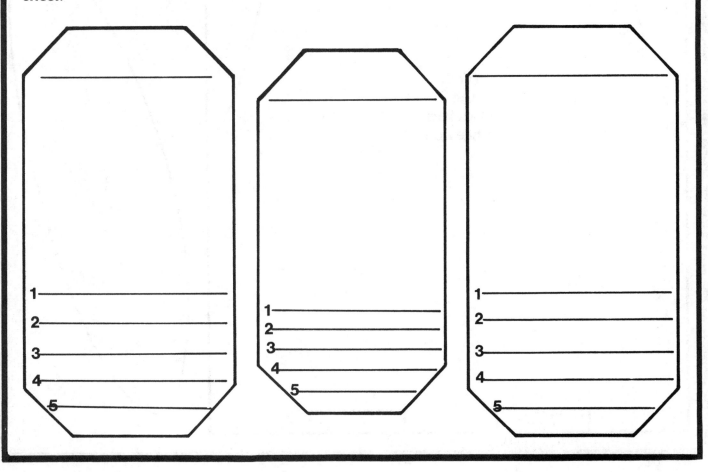

1 _____
2 _____
3 _____
4 _____
5 _____

1 _____
2 _____
3 _____
4 _____
5 _____

1 _____
2 _____
3 _____
4 _____
5 _____

Penguin Puppet

Use these pattern pieces to create your own penguin. Trace and cut out the pieces on construction paper. Glue edges only on the black and white body pieces, leaving the bottom open like a glove. Add a black tail to the back.

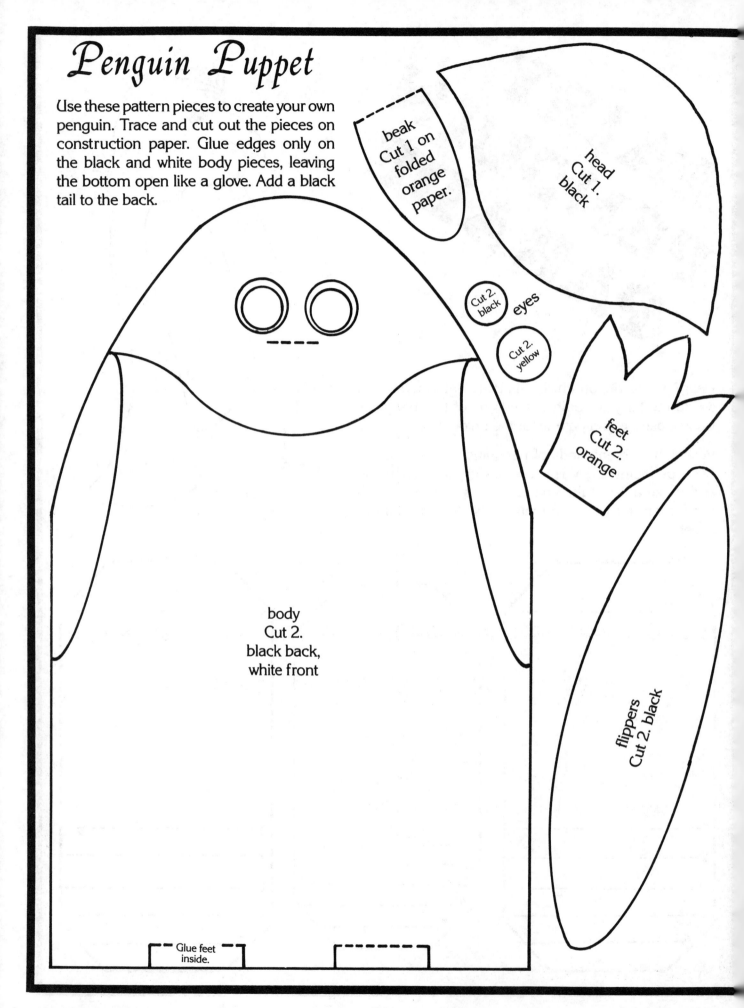

beak
Cut 1 on folded orange paper.

head
Cut 1.
black

Cut 2.
black   eyes

Cut 2.
yellow

feet
Cut 2.
orange

body
Cut 2.
black back,
white front

flippers
Cut 2. black

Glue feet inside.

14

AUSTRALIA

ZIPPIN' ON...

- Learn about the sport of cricket.

- Why were Captain James Cook, Captain Bligh and Captain Arthur Phillip important in Australia's history?

- Learn more about the unusual wildlife in Australia.

- Sydney's Opera House has a unique architecture. Who designed it?

- The Aborigines add their own celebrations and art forms. Learn more about them.

VALUABLE RESOURCES

Australian Tourist Commission. New York.

Constable, G. *Australia*. Amsterdam: Time-Life Books, 1985.

Lands and Peoples Encyclopedia. Danbury, CT: Grolier, 1987.

Terrill, R. *The Australians*. New York: Simon & Schuster, Inc., 1987.

GA1326

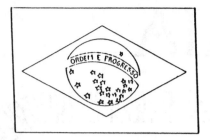
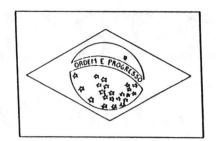
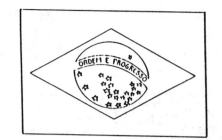

BRAZIL

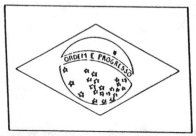
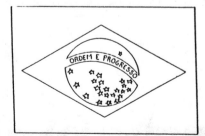
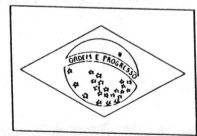

16

GA1326

Brazil makes up nearly half of the total area of South America. It borders every country in South America except Chile. Eastern Brazil has over 4000 miles (6436 km) of South Atlantic coastline and some of the most beautiful beaches in the world.

Brazil is almost totally in the Southern Hemisphere. The seasons are the direct opposite of those in Europe or the United States. The climate ranges from tropical in the north to a more temperate climate in the south.

The population of Brazil is approximately 130 million with 70 percent under the age of thirty.

The northern region is almost entirely covered by the Amazon Rain Forest. It is a region where the forest and rivers dictate the life-style of plants, animals and man. Much controversy continues as to the future of this delicate ecosystem.

1. São Paulo
2. Bahia
3. Pernambuco
4. Ceará
5. Brasília*
6. South America

BRAZIL

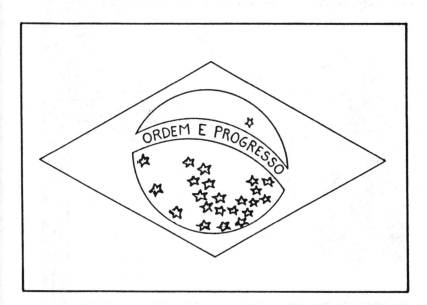

The national flag of the Federal Republic of Brazil was modified in 1968. It has à large yellow diamond in the center of a green field. In the center of the diamond is a blue globe representing the night sky. There are twenty-three stars representing the twenty-two states and the capital. Encircling the globe is a white banner stating the national motto: *Ordem e Progresso* meaning "Order and Progress."

GA1326

CARNIVAL

All of Brazil celebrates the world's most famous Carnival. The holiday originally came from the Shrove Tuesday commemoration in Portugal. During the simple, original celebration, people would be sprayed with cold water and flour.

Gradually Carnival has grown into a lengthy, massive holiday gala ending with the Cremation of Sadness. Brazilians, especially in Rio, participate in masquerades, enormous public theme balls, dancing in the streets, private dances at clubs and organized parades with thousands of dancers from samba schools. Samba "schools" are neighborhood clubs that organize a parade based on some theme of Brazilian history or folklore. The schools defend their colors with floats, a band, an original samba dance and two to three thousand costumed dancers who sing and dance and interpret their theme. The parade is lively and often begins one day and goes all night until the next day. Parade watchers often get caught up in the music and huge crowds join in the parade.

Elaborate costumes with much glitter, sequins, feathers and bright colors, mask the dancers. Often unusual hats become a major part of the costume.

Choose a theme from the following: Circus, Hawaii, Gold, Tropical Birds and Animals.

Design costumes for your samba dancers. Make sure the headpieces are large and fancy. If you have time, try designing a float to depict your theme choice.

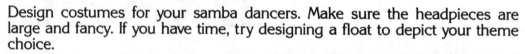

GA1326

CARNIVAL

MATERIALS

4″ x 12″ (10.16 x 30.48 cm) heavy
   paper
construction paper for eyes, nose, etc.
2 12″ (30.48 cm) pieces of ribbon,
   yarn or string

OPTIONAL

glitter
yarn
sequins
feathers

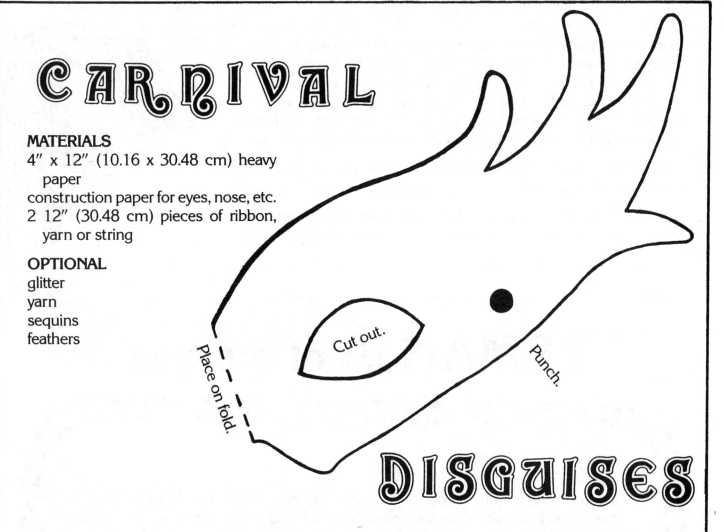

Place on fold.

Cut out.

Punch.

DISGUISES

Use the mask pattern to make a disguise for Carnival. Fold heavy paper in half and trace the mask pattern. Cut out the mask and eyeholes. Punch the holes to attach a ribbon or string for wearing.

Fancy eyes can be glued to the basic mask. Color, glitter edges (not near the eye openings) or fill in the space with yarn. Eyelashes, eyebrows, nose, etc., can be added. Real feathers or the feather pattern can be used to add additional glamour.

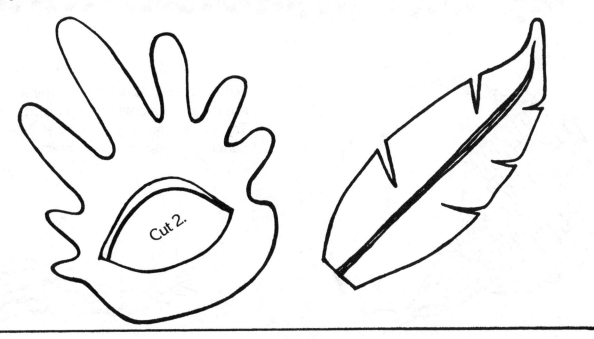

Cut 2.

GA1326

The state of Bahia on the eastern coast of Brazil holds an Afro-Brazilian religious celebration on the twelfth of October. Processions of *candomblé* (religious followers) bring presents to *Lemanjá* (goddess). She is the supernatural being who lives in the sea. The processioners bring gifts of flowers, mirrors, fans, combs and perfumes to her. Songs are sung in Lemanjá's honor.

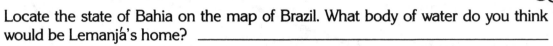

Locate the state of Bahia on the map of Brazil. What body of water do you think would be Lemanjá's home? _____

Think about the location of this state. Think about people who live near an ocean. Why would they want to keep the goddess of the sea happy?

_____

_____

LEMANJÁ of the Sea

Use the melody to the song, "By the Sea, by the Sea, by the Beautiful Sea" to write a song that would honor Lemanjá. When you begin, you may want to first list words that are synonyms for *honor*; then add words that describe the sea; and finally, include words that describe the goddess.

In the seashell, draw what you think Lemanjá looks like as she accepts the gifts from the Brazilians. Try to use as many real seashell shapes and patterns as you can in your picture.

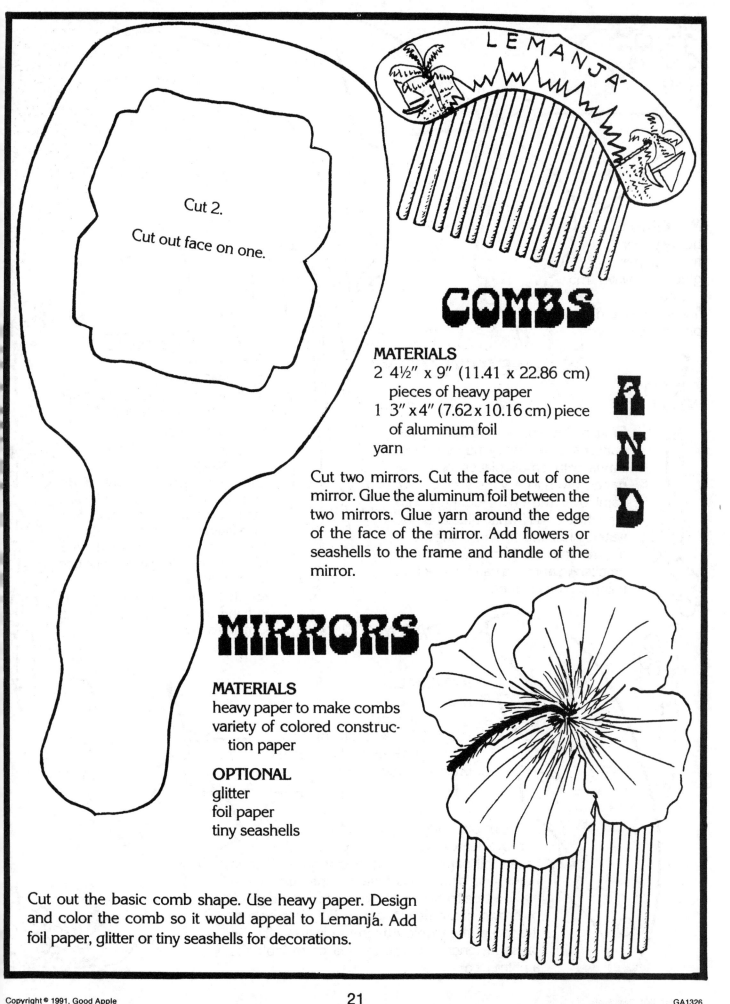

Cut 2.

Cut out face on one.

COMBS

MATERIALS
2 4½″ x 9″ (11.41 x 22.86 cm)
   pieces of heavy paper
1 3″ x 4″ (7.62 x 10.16 cm) piece
   of aluminum foil
yarn

Cut two mirrors. Cut the face out of one mirror. Glue the aluminum foil between the two mirrors. Glue yarn around the edge of the face of the mirror. Add flowers or seashells to the frame and handle of the mirror.

AND

MIRRORS

MATERIALS
heavy paper to make combs
variety of colored construction paper

OPTIONAL
glitter
foil paper
tiny seashells

Cut out the basic comb shape. Use heavy paper. Design and color the comb so it would appeal to Lemanjá. Add foil paper, glitter or tiny seashells for decorations.

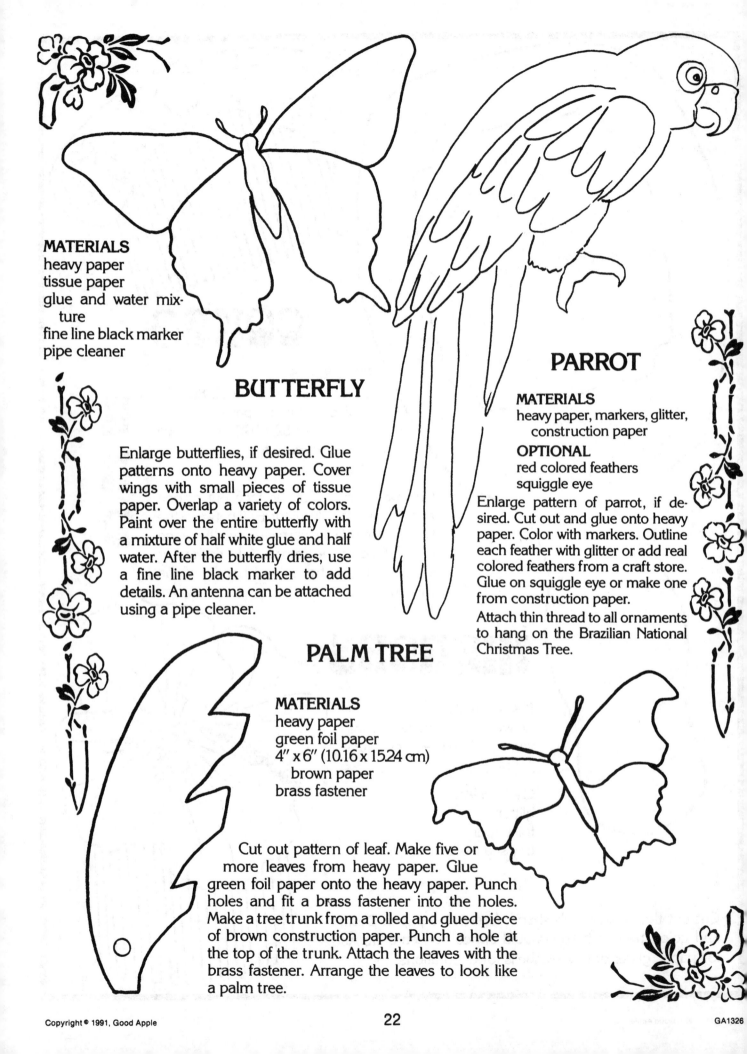

MATERIALS
heavy paper
tissue paper
glue and water mix-
ture
fine line black marker
pipe cleaner

BUTTERFLY

Enlarge butterflies, if desired. Glue patterns onto heavy paper. Cover wings with small pieces of tissue paper. Overlap a variety of colors. Paint over the entire butterfly with a mixture of half white glue and half water. After the butterfly dries, use a fine line black marker to add details. An antenna can be attached using a pipe cleaner.

PARROT

MATERIALS
heavy paper, markers, glitter,
construction paper
OPTIONAL
red colored feathers
squiggle eye

Enlarge pattern of parrot, if desired. Cut out and glue onto heavy paper. Color with markers. Outline each feather with glitter or add real colored feathers from a craft store. Glue on squiggle eye or make one from construction paper.

Attach thin thread to all ornaments to hang on the Brazilian National Christmas Tree.

PALM TREE

MATERIALS
heavy paper
green foil paper
4″ x 6″ (10.16 x 15.24 cm)
brown paper
brass fastener

Cut out pattern of leaf. Make five or more leaves from heavy paper. Glue green foil paper onto the heavy paper. Punch holes and fit a brass fastener into the holes. Make a tree trunk from a rolled and glued piece of brown construction paper. Punch a hole at the top of the trunk. Attach the leaves with the brass fastener. Arrange the leaves to look like a palm tree.

GA1326

Christmas in Brazil is a festival blend of African, Indian and Portuguese-Catholic customs.

In the states of Ceará, Pernambuco and Bahia, there are elaborate pageants, folk plays, satirical dramas, singing and dancing. The fandango and cheganca are popular dances along with the samba.

In southern Brazil, European and American traditions have replaced the Brazilian ones. Even though Christmas is in the middle of Brazil's summer, Papai Noel (Santa Claus) arrives in black boots and a red flannel suit.

Papai Noel

Decorate this traditional European Christmas tree to represent Brazil. Some ornament suggestions are orchids, fans, parrots, fish, coffee cups, alligators and butterflies. Papai Noel should be in your picture, also.

You need to use bright colors and create "sparkle."

GA1326

FESTA DA APARECIDA

Throughout the month of September millions of Brazilians travel to São Paulo to visit the grotto of Lady of Aparecida. She was a black patron saint of São Paulo. She is believed to have miraculous powers. During this visit, millions appeal to her to perform miracles for them.

WHAT DO YOU THINK. . . ?

1. What do the Brazilian people ask for?

2. What would you ask her for that would take a miracle?

3. Do you know of someone that people in your country go to for special favors?

4. What kind of miracle do you think Lady of Aparecida performed that made her a patron saint?

  Using your imagination and the information you know about the people of Brazil, write an imaginary folktale. In this story tell when, where, why and how the Miracle of Lady of Aparecida occurred. Include names of people and places in Brazil.

GA1326

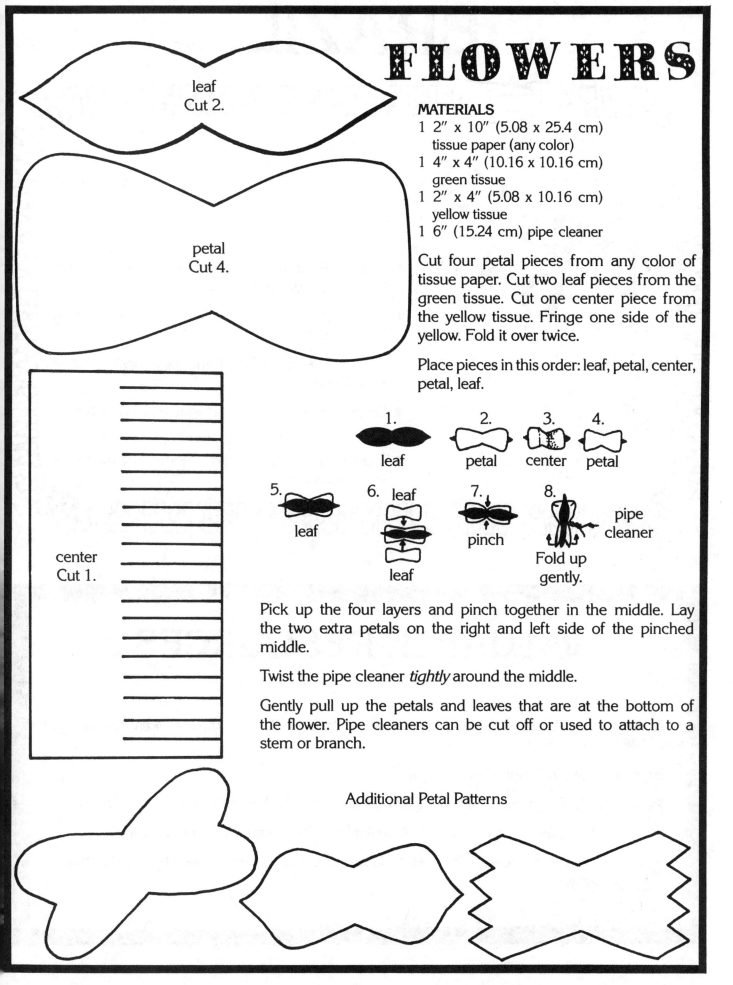

FLOWERS

leaf
Cut 2.

petal
Cut 4.

center
Cut 1.

MATERIALS

1 2″ x 10″ (5.08 x 25.4 cm)
 tissue paper (any color)
1 4″ x 4″ (10.16 x 10.16 cm)
 green tissue
1 2″ x 4″ (5.08 x 10.16 cm)
 yellow tissue
1 6″ (15.24 cm) pipe cleaner

Cut four petal pieces from any color of tissue paper. Cut two leaf pieces from the green tissue. Cut one center piece from the yellow tissue. Fringe one side of the yellow. Fold it over twice.

Place pieces in this order: leaf, petal, center, petal, leaf.

1. leaf
2. petal
3. center
4. petal
5. leaf
6. leaf / leaf
7. pinch
8. pipe cleaner / Fold up gently.

Pick up the four layers and pinch together in the middle. Lay the two extra petals on the right and left side of the pinched middle.

Twist the pipe cleaner *tightly* around the middle.

Gently pull up the petals and leaves that are at the bottom of the flower. Pipe cleaners can be cut off or used to attach to a stem or branch.

Additional Petal Patterns

GA1326

BRAZIL

ZIPPIN' ON...

- Learn the samba, the fandango or the cheganca from a local dance studio.

- Draw pictures of Santa Claus as he is depicted in different countries.

- Learn more about Brazil and its struggle to save the rain forest.

- Learn some words in Portuguese, Brazil's official language.

- Work in groups, each with a theme, and have your own carnival parade.

VALUABLE RESOURCES

Angelich, A. "Where carnival is hot—Rio de Janeiro, Brazil." *Travel-Holiday* (February 1984), pp. 62-65, 82.

Brazilian Tourism Foundation. New York.

Kurian, G. T. *Encyclopedia of the Third World* (Vol. 1). New York: Facts on File, 1987.

Lands and Peoples—Central & South America (Vol. 6). Danbury, CT: Grolier, 1987.

Weil, T. E. *Brazil: A Country Study.* U. S. Government study represented by the Secretary of the Army, 1983.

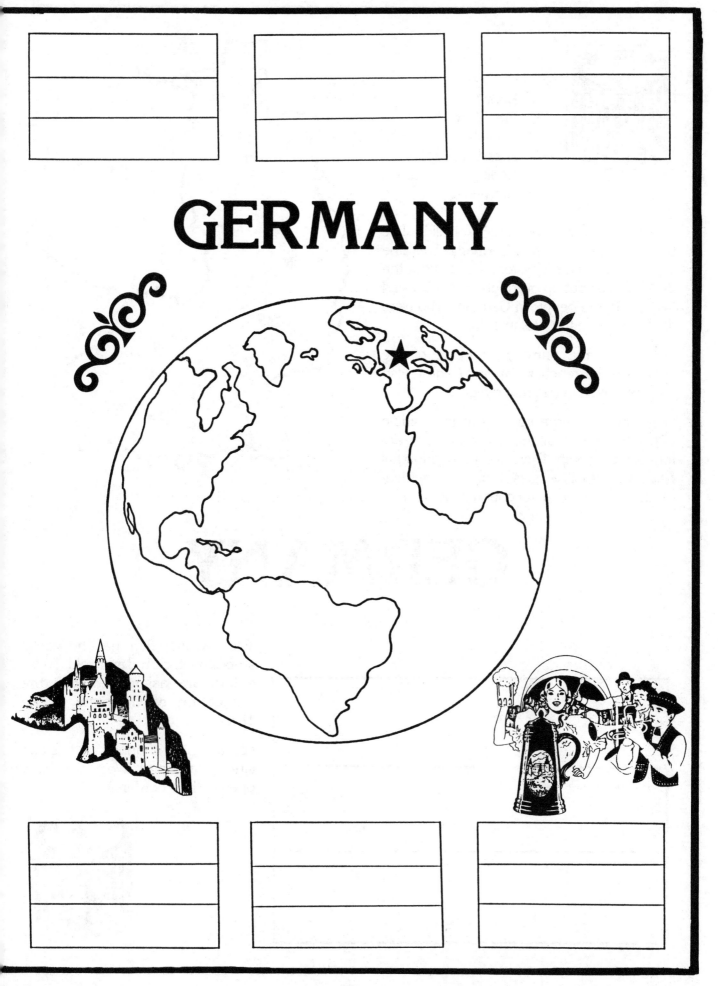

GERMANY

GA1326

1. Bonn*
2. Frankfurt
3. Munich
4. Dresden
5. Berlin
6. Bremen

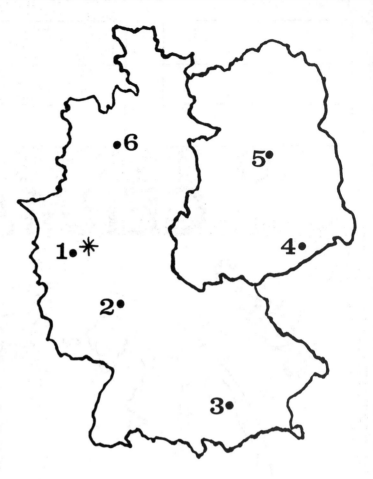

On this map you will see a dividing line between East and West Germany. That line is part of Germany's history. Read about the Wall that was put up overnight in 1945. Read also about the people in Germany who were able to remove the Wall in 1990.

Deutsch is the primary language of the country with French, Italian and English also readily spoken in different regions.

Germany is a large country in the middle of Europe. The beautiful Alps mountains are found in the south. There are many industrial cities and small villages, too. Many ancient castles dot the beautiful countryside.

GERMANY

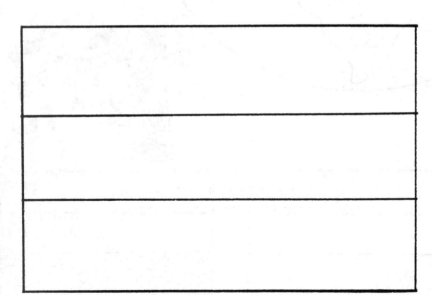

The national flag has horizontal stripes of black, red and gold. These colors are associated with the unification of Germany in the 1830's.

Has anything changed on this flag since East and West Germany opened their borders?

GA132

O TANNENBAUM

Germany is credited with introducing the evergreen tree to the Christmas celebration. There are several legends, but the most familiar is about Martin Luther, a leader in the religious Reformation. It is said that as he was walking home from church on a clear, starry night, he was awed by the beauty. He wanted to share this special scene with his family. He brought into the house a small fir tree, added gold and silver stars and put tiny candles on the tips of the branches. The German legend states this is how the first Christmas tree came to be.

There are other German legends about the first Christmas tree and the Advent calendar. Try to find more information about these legends.

30

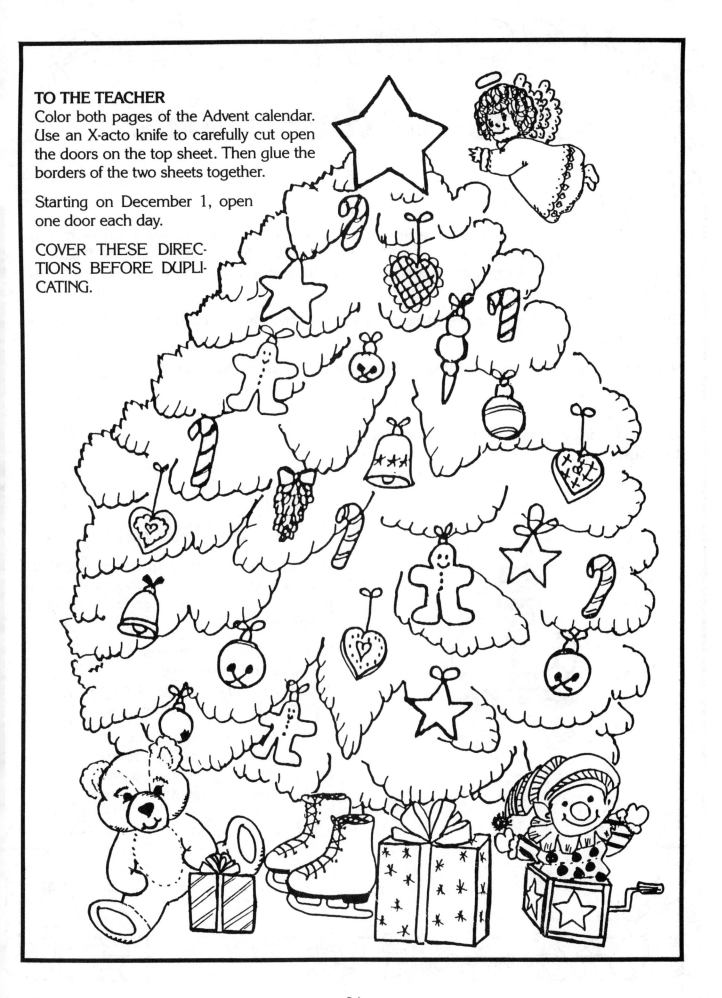

TO THE TEACHER
Color both pages of the Advent calendar.
Use an X-acto knife to carefully cut open
the doors on the top sheet. Then glue the
borders of the two sheets together.

Starting on December 1, open
one door each day.

COVER THESE DIREC-
TIONS BEFORE DUPLI-
CATING.

31

Christkindlesmarkt

The Christmas holiday begins in early December with the *Christkindlesmarkt* or toy fair in Nuremberg. This market is huge and held outdoors. Shoppers can shop for wooden toys from the Black Forest area, mechanical toys from Germany's toy factories and toys imported from all over the world.

There are also gingerbread figures, glass ornaments of tiny animals and figures made of sugary marzipan dough.

While the shopping goes on, Christmas carolers and bands add to the festive air.

Design a toy below that a small child would enjoy receiving for Christmas.

Marzipan

Use the recipe below to make your own marzipan creations. Often these figures are placed on sticks like suckers. Use your imagination!

8 oz. (226.79 g) almond paste
¼ cup (60 ml) corn syrup
¾ cup (180 ml) marshmallow creme
1 lb. (473.18 ml) confectioners' sugar

Combine ingredients; blend with hands. Form into shapes of toys, ornaments or animals. Paint with food coloring dissolved in water.

GA1326

The most famous festival in Germany is Oktoberfest held in Munich. It begins in late September and goes into October.

The first Oktoberfest was held in 1810 to celebrate the marriage of King Ludwig I of Bavaria to Princess Therese von Sachsen Hilburghausen.

The first Sunday in Oktoberfest marks the day of a huge parade with elaborate floats sponsored by the German beer companies. Marksmen, folklore groups and ethnic dancers join the parade in colorful Bavarian lederhosen and dirndl dresses.

The Munich fairgrounds, known as Theresa Meadows, is crowded with tens of thousands of people and huge beer tents. Food is also a big part of the celebration. Roasted chicken, fish grilled on sticks and sausages galore abound for the festival-goers. There are also sideshows, rides, brass bands and dancing.

- You may want to have your own Oktoberfest. Act out the plays of the Grimm Brothers such as "Snow White" and "Hansel and Gretel." Serve root beer, pretzels, sausages and sauerkraut, or frankfurters. Have hand-decorated gingerbread cookies for desert. Set up a miniature golf area with famous German landmarks. Sing German songs and dance the polka!

- Create a map below of the Munich fairgrounds. Where are the food stands, the band stands, the rides, etc.? What other facilities are needed at a large gathering like this? Add them to your map.

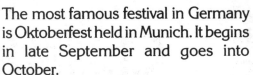

OKTOBERFEST

Richard Wagner
Music Festival

During the months of July and August, the city of Bayreuth hosts the internationally known Wagner Music Festival. During this time the famous German composer Richard Wagner is honored. His famous operas are performed nightly for music lovers. Germany has fostered many famous composers whose works are still honored and recognized as geniuses.

- Research these well-known composers and list their most famous works. If a music audio library is available to you, listen to a famous work from each of these artists. What is your reaction to this music?

German Composer	Name of Composition	Your Reaction

- Can you take a simple melody from any of these works and write your own words or poetry to go with it?

34

GA1326

FIRST DAY of SCHOOL

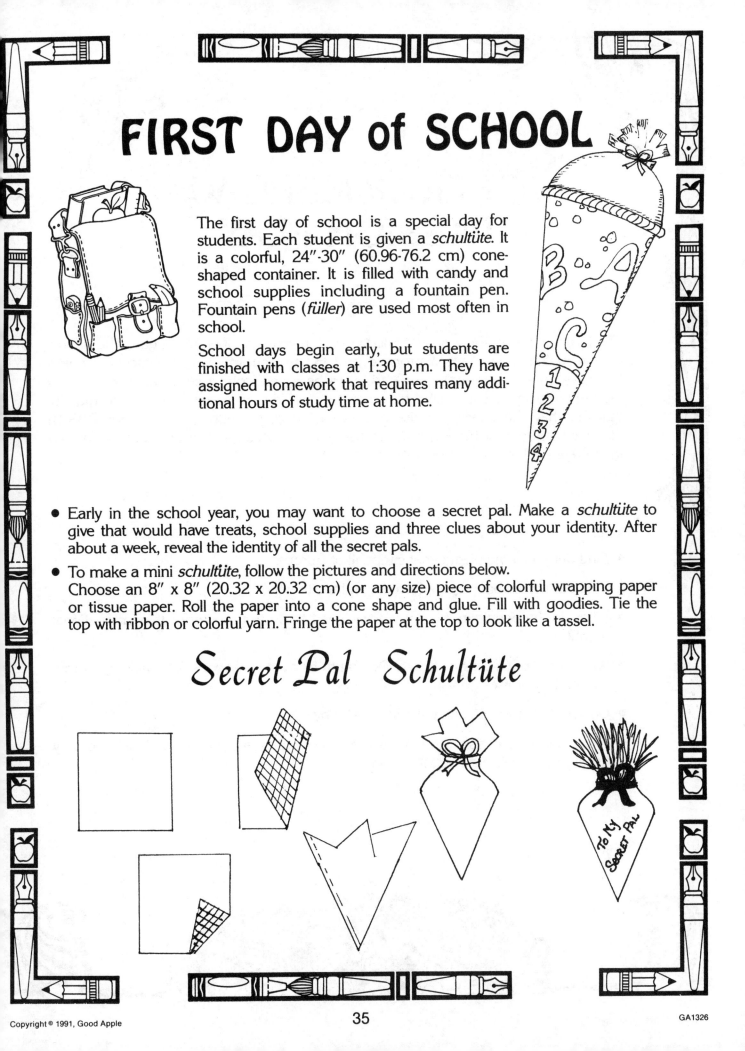

The first day of school is a special day for students. Each student is given a *schultüte*. It is a colorful, 24″-30″ (60.96-76.2 cm) cone-shaped container. It is filled with candy and school supplies including a fountain pen. Fountain pens (*füller*) are used most often in school.

School days begin early, but students are finished with classes at 1:30 p.m. They have assigned homework that requires many additional hours of study time at home.

- Early in the school year, you may want to choose a secret pal. Make a *schultüte* to give that would have treats, school supplies and three clues about your identity. After about a week, reveal the identity of all the secret pals.

- To make a mini *schultüte*, follow the pictures and directions below.
  Choose an 8″ x 8″ (20.32 x 20.32 cm) (or any size) piece of colorful wrapping paper or tissue paper. Roll the paper into a cone shape and glue. Fill with goodies. Tie the top with ribbon or colorful yarn. Fringe the paper at the top to look like a tassel.

Secret Pal Schultüte

GA1326

OBERAMMERGAU PASSION PLAY

The famous Passion Play is performed every ten years in Oberammergau. The people of this Alpine town made a promise in 1633 to perform a play depicting Christ's last days on earth. In return they asked to be saved from a sure death inflicted by the terrible plague. The legend tells that the people were saved and were so grateful that they have kept their promise and every ten years perform the famous Passion Play for hundreds of thousands of international spectators. The play was performed in 1990 and the promise was again fulfilled.

- Find out about the plague that swept all of Europe.

- Find out more about the performers and the theater.

- What do the people in this small town need to do to prepare for this international event?

- What is the price of each ticket? Do you think the townspeople are making a profit off of this promise?

- Do you think the tradition will continue? Why?

- What kind of promises do people make when they are asking for help? Do they usually keep their promises for a long time?

36

GA1326

GERMANY

ZIPPIN' ON...

- Research the famous stories of the Grimm Brothers.

- St. Nicholas Day is also a favorite holiday. Learn more about the legend of St. Nicholas.

- Carnival in Cologne, Germany, is always colorful. Find out how it is celebrated.

- Easter is another holiday celebrated. Find out what *osterschinken* is and how it is used at the festivities.

- Maitag or Walpurgis Night is similar to Halloween.

- St. Martin's Festival is held in November and harvesttime. How is harvest celebrated?

- Green Thursday is called Gründonnerstag. Why?

VALUABLE RESOURCES

Do You Know Germany? New York: German Information Center, 1989.

Fairclough, C. *Take a Trip to West Germany.* New York: Franklin Watts, 1981.

Römer, K. *Facts About Germany.* Munich: Lexikon-Institut Bertelsmann, 1987.

GA1326

GREAT BRITAIN

38

GA1326

GREAT BRITAIN

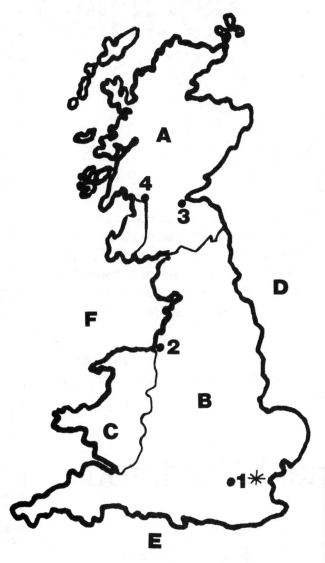

The Union flag is a combination of the main parts of the United Kingdom flags, except Wales.

The flag of England is represented by the center red cross. The flag of Scotland adds the blue field. The flag of Wales is divided horizontally, white over green with a red dragon in the center. It was not added to the Union flag.

1. London*
2. Liverpool
3. Edinburgh
4. Glasglow

A. Scotland
B. England
C. Wales
D. North Sea
E. English Channel
F. Irish Sea

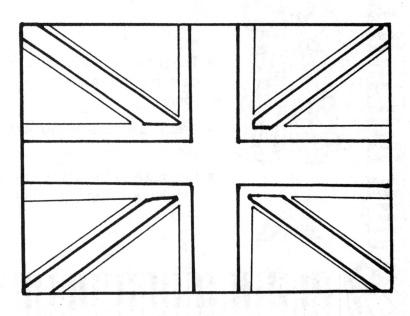

GA1326

Many ancient traditions are kept alive in Wales. The National Eisteddfod, which is a music and poetry festival, is a celebration and reason for wearing traditional costumes. The celebration is held annually and a *bard* is chosen. Poetry is created and read at the celebration with poets hoping theirs will be considered the quality accepted by the judges. A new bard (famous poet) is chosen only if a poem, dance or music reaches the high standards set at the National Eisteddfod.

The contest is held in a different locality each year. The judges are robed in different colors to represent their years of experience. Green robes are the novices, blue are the intermediates and white are the masters.

National Eisteddfod

- Teach the rest of your group or class how to write a fourteen-line sonnet.

- Create a dance to go with the poem.

- Compose simple music, perhaps with kazoos. Tape the whole production.

40

GA1326

Guy Fawkes Day

Guy Fawkes Day is celebrated on November 5 in England. This day commemorates Guy Fawkes who was one of the conspirators who attempted to kill King James I in 1605. This attempt, known as the Gunpowder Plot, was caused by the government's refusal to change its policy against Roman Catholics.

Fawkes and his small group planned to set fire to thirty-six barrels of gunpowder that were hidden in the cellar of the House of Lords. A Catholic associate was told not to attend the opening session of Parliament that day. He became suspicious and reported the information to the police. Fawkes's plan was never carried out. The conspirators were caught and executed.

Guy Fawkes Day is celebrated with bonfires and a parade of lanterns and music. In the parade an effigy called *The Guy* is carried to a huge bonfire. There it is set on fire and burned. Fireworks displays also light the evening sky.

- Using the information about Guy Fawkes and his plan, write and present an on-the-spot news report about the event.

- Produce a big book for young students. Be sure your information and illustrations are acurate in this storybook.

NOV. 5

GA1326

Shrove Tuesday

In Great Britain the last Tuesday before Lent begins is designated as *Shrove Tuesday*. It is known in other countries as *Fastnacht, Mardi Gras* and *Carnival*. Wild football games are played, traditional foods are eaten, parades and parties are enjoyed. One traditional food served is pancakes. In fact this day is also known as Pancake Day!

One of the highlights of the day is when the women of the local town race to the church when they hear the bells ringing. Each carries a skillet with pancakes inside. Legend tells that over 500 years ago a woman was preparing pancakes for her family when she heard the bells ringing. In her haste, she forgot to take off her apron and raced to the church with the skillet still in her hand. The next year more women did the same thing. Whoever reached the church first would get a kiss from the bell ringer. This was called the Kiss of Peace. Racers now continue this tradition and must flip their pancakes at the starting line and again at the finish line to prove they still have them!

- Prepare pancakes for your class. You may want to try this race just for fun.

- Plan several relay races using kitchen utensils and food, real or paper.

- Pantomime the race with a group of your friends.

- Design a poster advertising this pancake race.

GA1326

Boxing Day

Boxing Day is a national holiday in England. It is celebrated on December 26. Legend tells that on this day the noblemen "boxed up" gifts for their servants.

Boxing Day is also called St. Stephen's Day. St. Stephen was a martyr who was stoned to death. Boxes that were placed in the churches throughout the year are opened this day. Payment for special services that were done during the year are distributed on this day. Children also go from house to house asking for contributions.

- Collect canned goods for your local food pantry. Collect used clothing for needy families. Decorate the collection boxes and prepare information sheets about your collections.

- Write a thank-you card or letter to someone who has helped.

HOGMANAY

One of Scotland's most important festivals is Hogmanay. It is celebrated on New Year's Day. Many locals wear their traditional costumes. Special Scottish music is played and whiskey is consumed at the festivities.

- Learn how to dance the Scottish reel.

- Research bagpiping.

- Make a line drawing in the box. Use one continuous line. Show a Scottish bagpiper.

GA1326

Halloween

Harvest festivals lead to the **Halloween** celebration on October 31. **Witch** hats are part of the **costumes** and children go from door to door announcing "**Trick** or **treat!**" **Pumpkin** lanterns are **carved** to scare away the real witches! **Parades**, **pranks**, **bonfires** and **games** are part of the celebration.

All Soul's Day was the original celebration but was not permitted by the Roman Catholic Church. Protestants kept some of the original customs of **praying** for the souls of the dead.

Another similar celebration is **Plough Day**. On this day the Ploughmen went **begging** for gifts. If they did not receive any, they threatened damage to the grounds with their ploughs.

- Design a Halloween board game.
- Create a Halloween bingo game using the bold words in the information above.

Braemar Games

The Braemar Royal Highland Gathering takes place in Scotland at the beginning of September. It is the most famous Highland Gathering of all, and the Royal Family is always in attendance. The men wear kilts representing their clans and participate in many feats of strength. One of the famous events is the toss of *cabers*. These are the trunks of trees often 15 to 20 feet (4.56 to 6.08 m) long and weighing over 100 pounds (45 kilograms). Judges measure the distance the trees are thrown. There is much merrymaking that goes on at this famous event. Highland bands play and march on the field where the contests are being held. *Lassies* or Scottish girls dance to the melodies of the bagpipers.

- Organize your own Highland Gathering. You might want to toss broomsticks, have a tug-o-war, etc.
- Draw a mural showing all of the events in the Braemer Royal Highland Gathering.
- Write a sports article for a newspaper describing the events and the winners.

GA1326

GREAT BRITAIN

ZIPPIN' ON...

There are more holidays celebrated in some parts of Great Britain.

Research the legends and modern celebrations still held.

- Easter
- Whit Sunday
- Village Fairs

- Carnival
- May Day
- Puck Fair in Ireland

VALUABLE RESOURCES

British Tourist Authority (for England, Scotland and Wales). New York.

Constable, G. *Britain*. Amsterdam: Time-Life Books, 1986.

Langley, A. *Passport to Great Britain*. New York: Franklin Watts, 1986.

Sproule, A. *Great Britain—The Land and Its People*. Morristown, NJ: Silver Burdett, 1986.

Tourtellot, J. *Discovering Britain and Ireland*. Washington, D.C.: National Geographic Society, 1985.

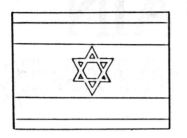 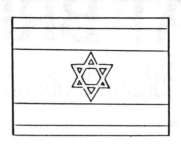 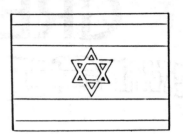

ISRAEL

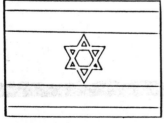 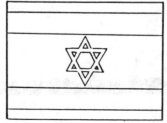 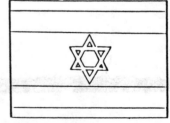

GA1326

ISRAEL

1. Golan Heights
2. Nazareth
3. Jericho
4. Jerusalem*
5. Bethlehem
6. Gaza
7. Tel Aviv
8. Haifa

A. Sea of Galilee
B. Dead Sea
C. Mediterranean Sea

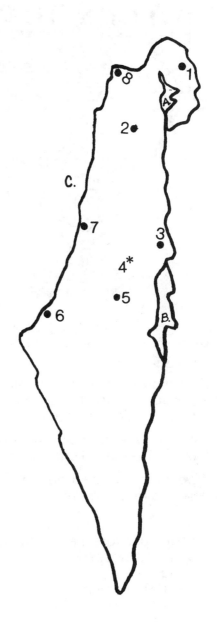

Israel's flag is a design of Yale blue and white stripes representing the Jewish prayer shawl. In the center, on a white field, is the six-pointed Star of David.

This flag was adopted by the new state of Israel in 1948.

Hanukkah
Festival of Lights

The Festival of Lights holiday, called Hanukkah, usually comes in December. It is an historical holiday.

Long ago the Jewish people rebelled against a Syrian king. They retook the Temple of Jerusalem. They reworked it and when it was ready, they had a rededication of this special temple. The celebration would use a vessel of oil. There was only enough oil for the lamp to burn one day, but amazingly, it stayed lit for eight days.

Now during Hanukkah, one candle is lighted on the eight-branch menorah to represent the oil lamp. Each day another candle is lit. In some Jewish homes there is feasting and gift exchanging as well as religious services on these eight days.

During the week of Hanukkah, work continues as usual but evenings are filled with songs, puzzles, riddles and games. Games of cards and "dreydl" (dreidl) are all part of the entertainment.

A favorite food served during Hanukkah is *latkes* or potato pancakes. Try the recipe below for a delicious treat. This recipe should be done with adult supervision.

Potato Latkes for Hanukkah

4 large potatoes, peeled and grated
¼ onion, chopped
2 eggs
¼ c. (60 ml) flour

1 tsp. (5 ml) salt
¼ tsp. (1.25 ml) pepper
¼ tsp. (1.25 ml) baking powder
oil for frying

In large bowl, place grated potatoes, onion and eggs. Stir to mix. Add flour, salt, pepper and baking powder. Mix well. Heat about ½ cup (125 ml) oil in skillet. Drop mixture by spoonfuls into hot oil, flattening with a spoon. Cook until browned, about three minutes on each side. Drain on paper toweling. Makes about twenty-four small latkes. Serve with applesauce.

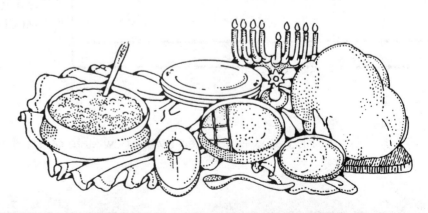

GA1326

Menorah Making

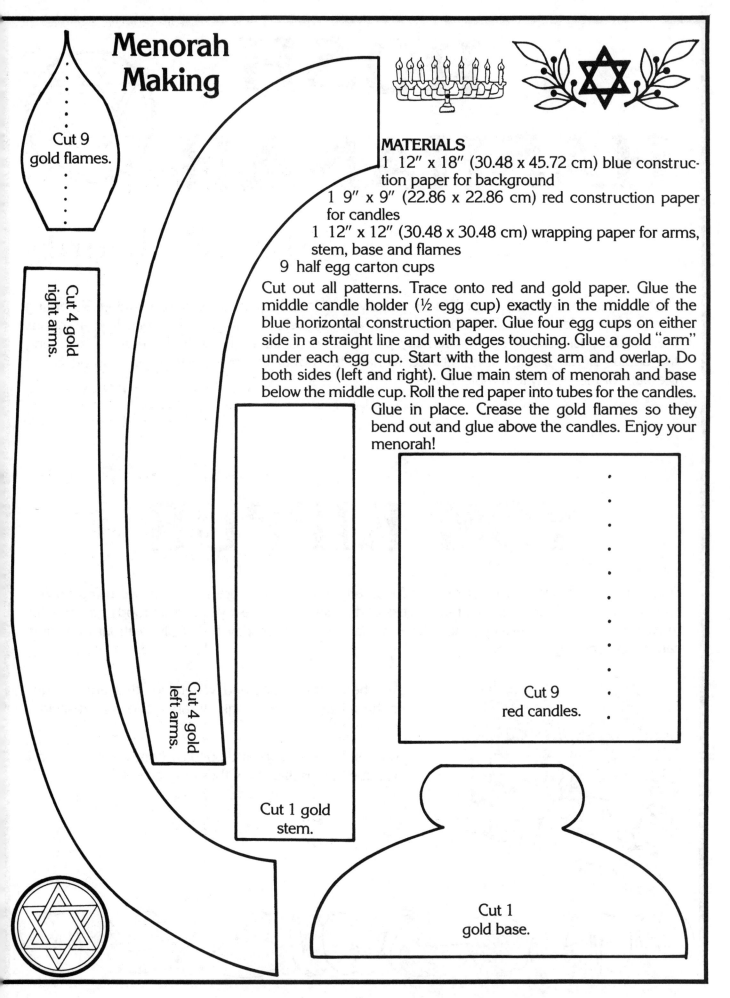

Cut 9
gold flames.

Cut 4 gold
right arms.

Cut 4 gold
left arms.

Cut 1 gold
stem.

MATERIALS

1 12" x 18" (30.48 x 45.72 cm) blue construction paper for background

1 9" x 9" (22.86 x 22.86 cm) red construction paper for candles

1 12" x 12" (30.48 x 30.48 cm) wrapping paper for arms, stem, base and flames

9 half egg carton cups

Cut out all patterns. Trace onto red and gold paper. Glue the middle candle holder (½ egg cup) exactly in the middle of the blue horizontal construction paper. Glue four egg cups on either side in a straight line and with edges touching. Glue a gold "arm" under each egg cup. Start with the longest arm and overlap. Do both sides (left and right). Glue main stem of menorah and base below the middle cup. Roll the red paper into tubes for the candles. Glue in place. Crease the gold flames so they bend out and glue above the candles. Enjoy your menorah!

Cut 9
red candles.

Cut 1
gold base.

GA1326

ROSH HASHANAH

Rosh Hashanah or Jewish New Year is usually held in either September or October according to the lunar calendar. Rosh Hashanah is not a noisy welcome to the new year. It is a serious look at the past year. There is a ten-day period of recollection. There is the ritual of sounding the *shofar* or ram's horn. It is believed to have the power to drive away evil spirits and cause the walls of the enemy to tumble down.

YOM KIPPUR

During this celebration no bitter or sour foods are served. There are many recipes using apples and honey. These foods represent sweetness and health for the next year. Other foods with special meaning include fish (fertility), the round *challah* or sweet holiday bread (life without end) and carrots (prosperity).

Are there other fruits and vegetables that are thought to have special meanings or are used for medicinal purposes?

Try taste testing apples dipped in honey. Can you find a recipe that uses both of these ingredients?

GA1326

Sukkot or Tabernacles is also known as the Festival of Booths. It comes eight days after the Day of Atonement. It is really a harvest festival and has an historical background. It is celebrated by Jews building booths of varied materials and decorated with fruits, vegetables and flowers. These booths symbolize the shelters built by Moses on his trip to the Promised Land. Meals are sometimes eaten in these booths along with singing, reading and enjoying each other's company.

The Sukkot celebration lasts for five days and occurs during September or October. There are synagogue services and the *kibbutzim* (collective settlement) celebrates with pageants, entertainment and displays of the community's harvested produce and newest manufactured goods.

SUKKOT

Festival of Booths

Many Jews make the pilgrimage to Jerusalem. Others enjoy the younger tradition of wine tasting.

Children enjoy carrying miniature sukkot on sticks as they march in parades.

Divide your class into three groups. Group 1 would construct a sukkot. Group 2 would decorate it with fruits, vegetables and flowers. They could be made of papier-mâche' or plastic. Group 3 should practice the reenactment of the story of Moses' journey.

GA1326

PASSOVER

Passover (Pessach) is also known as the Festival of Freedom. Passover is celebrated in either March or April depending on the lunar calendar.

The story is told that long ago the first born of each family was to die on an appointed night. However, if the door was marked with the blood of a lamb, the first born was spared. The Israelites were allowed to leave Egypt, and Passover commemorates this Exodus.

On the first and second nights of Passover, the Jews have a festive meal called the *seder*. The story of the Exodus is retold, songs are sung and everyone plays games. At the dinner table is an empty chair and glass of wine for the prophet Elijah.

To many Jews, Passover marks the birth of the nation of Israel.

Several favorite games played during Passover use nuts. These are a few simple games.

Passover Polo
A small circle is drawn on the floor. Peanuts are thrown into the circle. If an even number go in, player receives from banker the same number and the original nuts.

Player with the most peanuts at the end of the time wins.

Pessach Golf
Various places or holes are marked on the floor. Each player flips the peanut with thumb and forefinger to move it from hole to hole. Like golf, player with least amount of strokes is the winner.

Logging Nuts
Draw a line 10 to 20 feet (3.04 to 6.08 m) away from players. They stand at the line and throw peanuts. The one whose peanut is nearest the line wins all the other peanuts.

GA1326

✡ PURIM ✡

Purim is held in February or March and is one of the most joyous days in the Jewish religion. Purim recounts the events in the biblical book of Esther. Queen Esther found out there was an evil plan afoot by Haman. The plan would have all the Jews killed. Esther, who was a Jew, told the King and the lives of the Jews were saved.

Today, Purim is a national festival with much celebrating. There is much laughter and merrymaking. Children deliver special foods and wine to friends.

Children reenact the story of Esther with costumes. There are carnivals, costumed parades and public entertainment.

Purim is the Jewish answer to Mardi Gras.

Many Jews in coastal towns spend the day on the beaches rather than in the synagogues. There are also large crowds at football and other sporting events.

One of the favorite foods served during the Purim festival are poppy seed cookies. The recipe is below.

Poppy Seed Cookies

1 c. (250 ml) sugar
4 eggs
3 tsp. (15 ml) baking powder
1½ c. (375 ml) lukewarm water

1 c. (250 ml) salad oil
4 c. (960 ml) sifted flour
½ tsp. (2.5 ml) salt
¾ c. (180 ml) poppy seeds

Cream sugar and shortening. Add one egg at a time, stirring well. Sift dry ingredients and add poppy seeds. Combine both mixtures, adding a little water to form a stiff dough. Roll out on a lightly floured board—¼″ (.6 cm) thick. Cut into 2½″ (6.33 cm) triangles. Brush with egg yolk diluted with 1 tablespoon (15 ml) of water. Sprinkle mixture of poppy seeds and sugar on the cookies. Place on greased cookie sheet. Bake 350⁰ F (177⁰ C) for twelve to twenty-five minutes.

GA1326

CHRISTIAN HOLIDAYS

The Christian holidays that are celebrated in Israel include Christmas, Palm Sunday and Easter. The focus of the celebrations takes place in Jerusalem and Bethlehem. There are many tourists in Bethlehem during the Christmas season. Special services are held in the churches.

Palm Sunday and Easter are celebrated by walking the path Jesus walked.

The most important Muslim celebration occurs near Eastertime and lasts a whole month. The dates are determined by the ninth month of the Islamic calendar.

During this celebration there is no eating between sunrise and sunset.

It is a celebration of gratitude for receiving the Koran. It is the book containing Islamic law.

At the end of the fasting is a great feast. It is held at sunset on the last day.

It is traditional that the foods of the feast are shared with the poor.

MUSLIM HOLIDAYS

54

GA1326

ISRAEL

ZIPPIN' ON...

- Learn to play the dreidl game for Hanukkah.

- Find out about the Israeli Independence Day celebration held in May.

- Pentecost or Shavout is also an important holiday. When and how is it celebrated?

VALUABLE RESOURCES

Consulate General of Israel. Chicago: IL.

Constable, G. *Library of Nations—Israel.* Amsterdam: Time-Life Books, 1986.

Jones, H. H. *Enchantment of the World—Israel.* Chicago: Children's Press, 1986.

Zohar, D. *Israel—The Land and Its People.* London: Macdonald Educational Limited, 1989.

ITALY

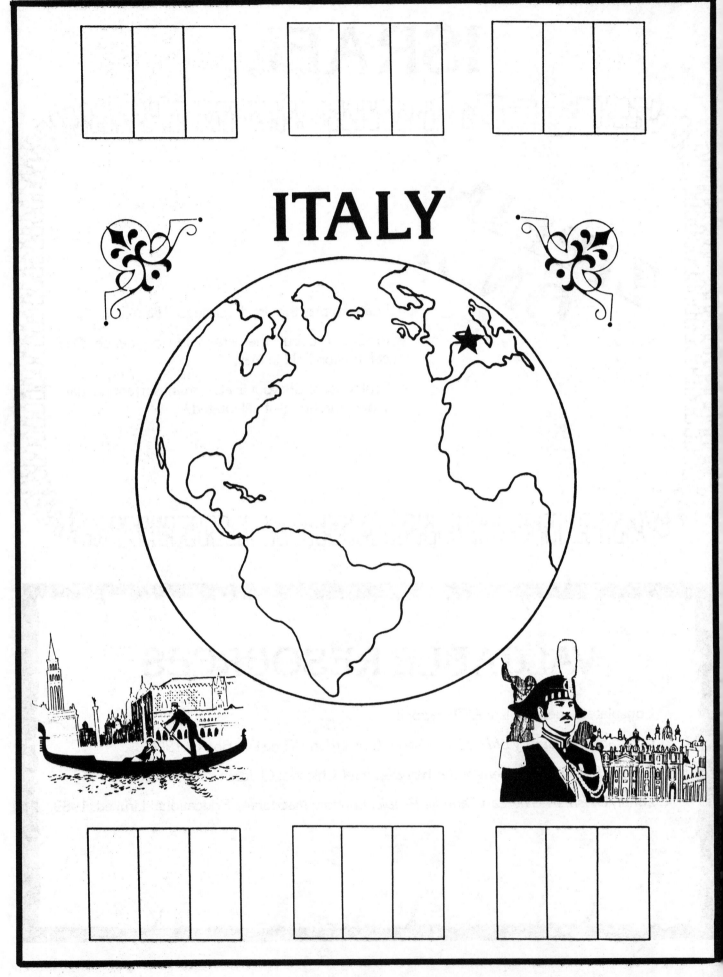

GA1326

ITALY

1. San Marino
2. Catanzaro
3. Naples
4. Rome*
5. Florence
6. Genoa
7. Milan
8. Venice
9. Ferrara

A. Adriactic Sea
B. Ionian Sea
C. Mediterranean Sea
D. Tyrrhenian Sea
E. Ligurian Sea
F. Sardinia
G. Sicily
H. Switzerland
I. Austria
J. Yugoslavia
K. France
L. Corsica

The tri-colored flag of Italy was adopted as the national flag in 1870. The vertical colors of green, white and red have been used in Italy's flags since the time of Napoleon.

The flag has been a symbol of freedom and unity for the Italian people.

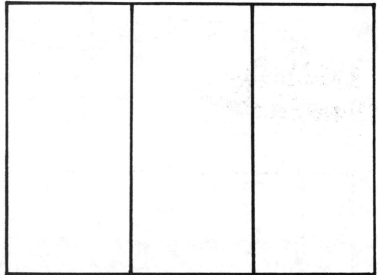

57

GA1326

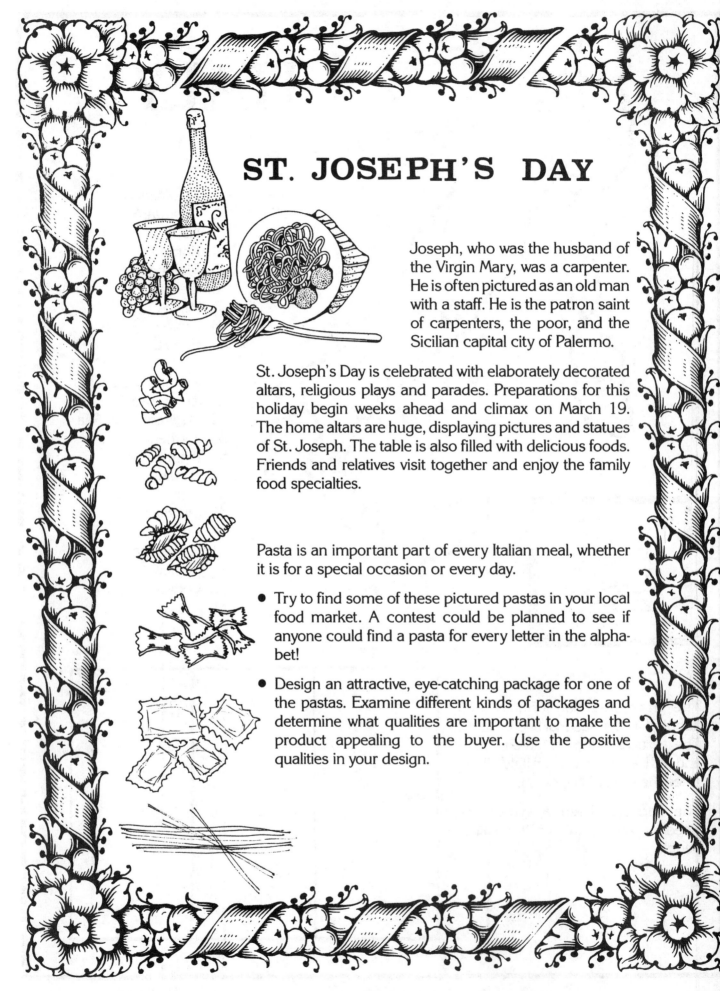

ST. JOSEPH'S DAY

Joseph, who was the husband of the Virgin Mary, was a carpenter. He is often pictured as an old man with a staff. He is the patron saint of carpenters, the poor, and the Sicilian capital city of Palermo.

St. Joseph's Day is celebrated with elaborately decorated altars, religious plays and parades. Preparations for this holiday begin weeks ahead and climax on March 19. The home altars are huge, displaying pictures and statues of St. Joseph. The table is also filled with delicious foods. Friends and relatives visit together and enjoy the family food specialties.

Pasta is an important part of every Italian meal, whether it is for a special occasion or every day.

- Try to find some of these pictured pastas in your local food market. A contest could be planned to see if anyone could find a pasta for every letter in the alphabet!

- Design an attractive, eye-catching package for one of the pastas. Examine different kinds of packages and determine what qualities are important to make the product appealing to the buyer. Use the positive qualities in your design.

PALIO

The Piazza del Campo, oval-shaped horse track, is in the center of Siena. The Palio (wild horse race) begins with a colorful parade with banner holders whirling and throwing them into the air like baton twirlers. Townspeople are dressed in costumes of the Middle Ages. Some men wear suits of armor.

An unusual ritual takes place before the horse race. Each church is decorated with flags, banners and signs displaying their winnings from previous races. The morning of the race, a church service is held and attended by the citizens backing that horse. The horse is also in the church. Silence and concentration on the horse are the important events. Everyone watches the behavior of the horse. These behaviors are considered omens about the horse's chances in winning. In fact, it is considered extremely good luck if the horse's droppings fall in the church. Often the priest will lengthen the church service in order to give the horse enough time to give this special omen.

The Palio ends with the wild horse race around the town square. The horses run at break-neck speeds often throwing off their jockeys. The winner's cup is presented to the horse finishing first. It does not need a rider! It is all over in two minutes!

- Mark off a square in the center of your classroom. Make three-legged horse teams. At the signal, try to race around the square as fast as you can. Present the winning "horse" with a ribbon and cup.

GA1326

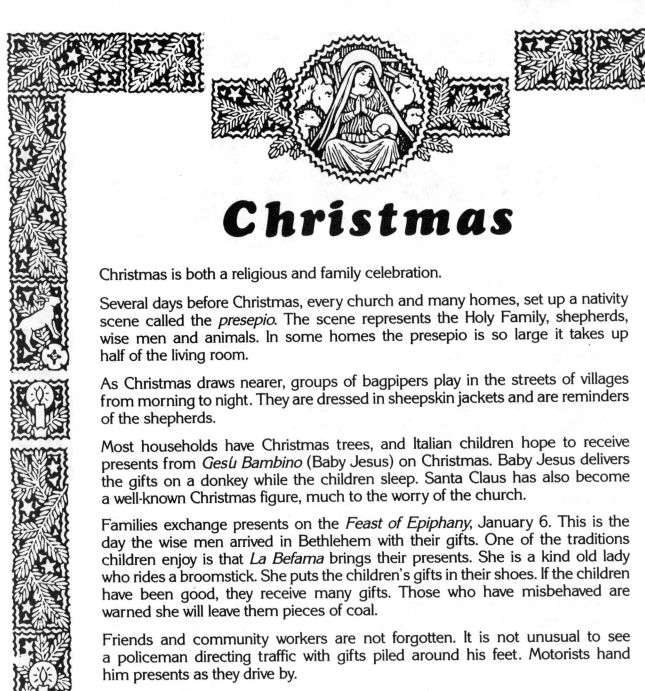

Christmas

Christmas is both a religious and family celebration.

Several days before Christmas, every church and many homes, set up a nativity scene called the *presepio*. The scene represents the Holy Family, shepherds, wise men and animals. In some homes the presepio is so large it takes up half of the living room.

As Christmas draws nearer, groups of bagpipers play in the streets of villages from morning to night. They are dressed in sheepskin jackets and are reminders of the shepherds.

Most households have Christmas trees, and Italian children hope to receive presents from *Gesù Bambino* (Baby Jesus) on Christmas. Baby Jesus delivers the gifts on a donkey while the children sleep. Santa Claus has also become a well-known Christmas figure, much to the worry of the church.

Families exchange presents on the *Feast of Epiphany*, January 6. This is the day the wise men arrived in Bethlehem with their gifts. One of the traditions children enjoy is that *La Befama* brings their presents. She is a kind old lady who rides a broomstick. She puts the children's gifts in their shoes. If the children have been good, they receive many gifts. Those who have misbehaved are warned she will leave them pieces of coal.

Friends and community workers are not forgotten. It is not unusual to see a policeman directing traffic with gifts piled around his feet. Motorists hand him presents as they drive by.

Special foods are always part of any Italian holiday. Christmas Eve is a fast day in the Roman Catholic religion. The family will eat fish that day and usually it is eel. The eel will be grilled or cooked in tomato sauce.

Panettone is also eaten at the end of the meal. It is the traditional Christmas cake made with raisins and citron. It is usually purchased and given as a gift to the hostess.

On Christmas Day a huge feast is eaten. Stuffed pasta, roasted turkey or veal, vegetables and cheeses are only a small part of the entire feast!

Presepio

MATERIALS

8½" x 11" (21.57 x 27.94 cm) turquoise tissue paper, 9" x 12" (22.86 x 30.48 cm) black construction paper, 2 8½" x 1" (21.57 x 2.54 cm) black strips, 2 11" x 1" (27.94 x 2.54 cm) black strips, gold star

1. Fold black strips lengthwise and glue to tissue paper edges to form a frame. 2. Cut out patterns. Trace onto black construction paper. Cut out. 3. Glue onto tissue paper. Glue gold star above the presepio.

OTHER OPTIONS

   a. Cut double black figures. Glue onto both sides of tissue.

   b. Make a gold foil frame. Glitter around edges of silhouettes.

   c. Add gold thread loop in center of top of frame for hanging.

EASTER

In Florence on Easter Eve, the church archbishop releases an artificial dove. It *flies* (with wires attached) to the church door. There it ignites a huge bonfire that was placed in a cart at the door. Fireworks explode as part of this religious festival.

On Easter Sunday, everyone enjoys Easter dinner with relatives. It is popular to eat roasted lamb and a special dove or cross-shaped cake. The cake is made with almonds and candied orange or lemon peel.

- Have a team contest. Decorate chocolate Easter eggs. Raffle the winning egg. *Sell* raffle tickets for work that is completed, perfect scores on assignments, returned homework, etc.

You can also sell the tickets for money in order to pay for the cost of producing the Easter eggs.

GA132

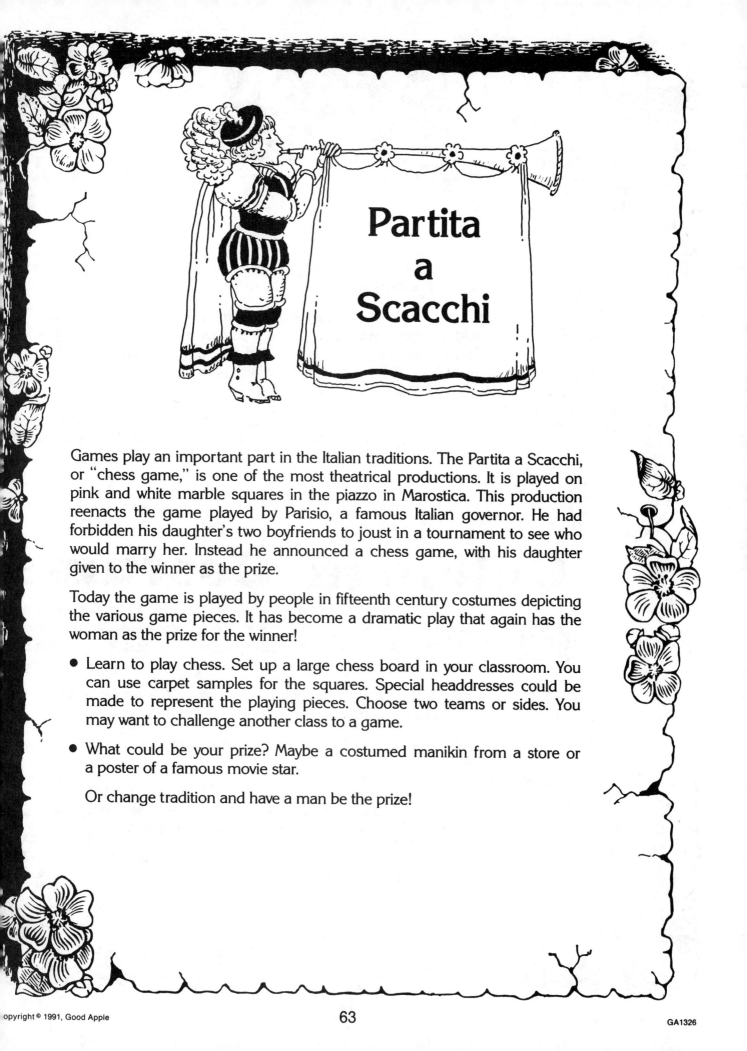

Partita a Scacchi

Games play an important part in the Italian traditions. The Partita a Scacchi, or "chess game," is one of the most theatrical productions. It is played on pink and white marble squares in the piazzo in Marostica. This production reenacts the game played by Parisio, a famous Italian governor. He had forbidden his daughter's two boyfriends to joust in a tournament to see who would marry her. Instead he announced a chess game, with his daughter given to the winner as the prize.

Today the game is played by people in fifteenth century costumes depicting the various game pieces. It has become a dramatic play that again has the woman as the prize for the winner!

- Learn to play chess. Set up a large chess board in your classroom. You can use carpet samples for the squares. Special headdresses could be made to represent the playing pieces. Choose two teams or sides. You may want to challenge another class to a game.

- What could be your prize? Maybe a costumed manikin from a store or a poster of a famous movie star.

  Or change tradition and have a man be the prize!

GA1326

Sagra

The smallest towns to the largest cities all enjoy a fair or *sagra*. The main event of these fairs is eating!

In Castel San Pietro, the Sagra della Braciòla (Fair of Mutton Chops) is held. Everyone attending gets a free mutton chop. The Ham Fair in San Daniele del Friuli sees that all those in attendance get thick slices of ham. The Festival of Spaghetti near Naples gives away huge portions of spaghetti with tomato sauce.

- Create a fair that would give away different kinds of pasta. What kinds of recipes would be used? Prepare some and share with the class!

Calcio in Costume

One of the oldest games played in Italy is Calcio in Costume or costumed soccer. It has been played in Florence since Roman times and is thought to be the basic game from which soccer was derived. It was a pastime for nobility who wore elegant costumes with silver and gold trimmings.

Around the turn of the eighteenth century, the game began to be played by the common people.

Today, the original Calcio in Costume is played once a year in grand style.

- Design a costume for the celebration that this modern soccer player could wear. Research what the nobility wore during Roman times.

  Would it be difficult to play soccer in this costume?

GA132

St. Anthony's Day

St. Anthony's Day is celebrated on June 13. St. Anthony came from Padua and became the patron saint of careless people. Those people may have lost an animal, a child or a valuable item.

The legend that goes with this holiday tells that St. Anthony's friend, St. Francis of Assisi, once preached to a fish when the congregation would not listen to his sermon.

In Rome, horses and mules are blessed. In Lisbon, the evening is spent enjoying bonfires and dancing.

- Have you ever lost something important to you?
  Did you find it?
  Did you ask anyone to help you find it?
  Why do you think horses and mules are blessed on this day in Rome?

ITALY

ZIPPIN' ON...

Research more of Italy's famous celebrations:

- famous bicycle race (Giro d' Italia)
- Italian Grand Prix Auto Race
- soccer competition
- typical Italian vacation
- St. Mark's Eve—April 25
- All Soul's Day
- Carnival Celebrations
- Ascension Day
- Miracle of San Gennaro
- Liberation Day—April 25

VALUABLE RESOURCES

Hubley, P., and J. Hubley. *A Family in Italy*. Minneapolis: Lerner Publications, 1986.

Italian Government Travel Office. New York.

Leech, M. *Italy—The Land and Its People*. London: Macdonald Educational Limited, 1984.

Mariella, C. *Passport to Italy*. New York: Franklin Watts, 1986.

GA132

KENYA

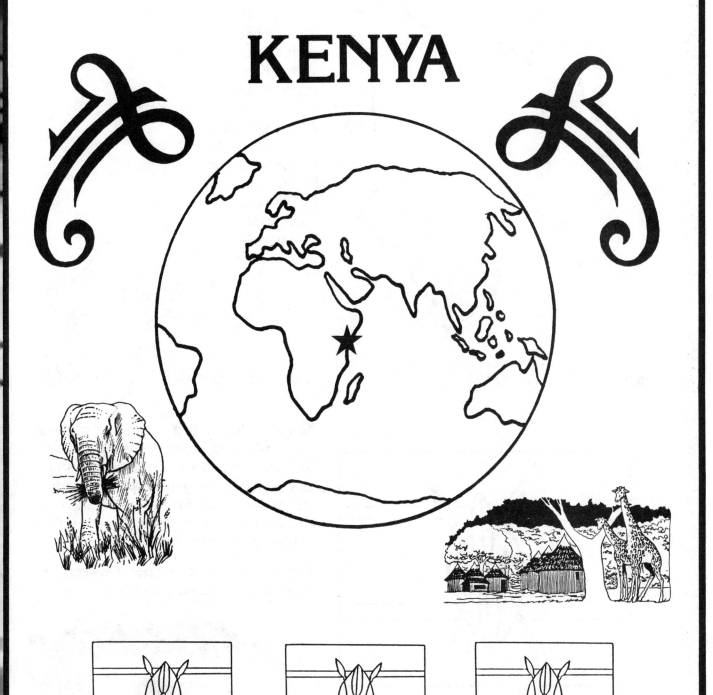

67

KENYA

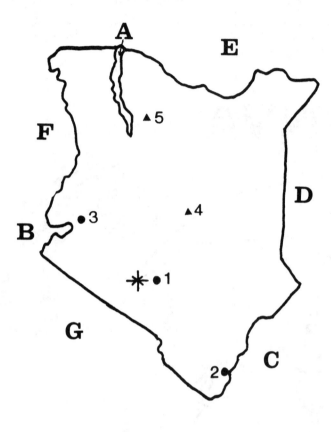

1. Nairobi*
2. Mombasa
3. Kisumu
4. Mt. Kenya
5. Mt. Kulal

A. Lake Turkana
B. Lake Victoria
C. Indian Ocean
D. Somalia
E. Ethiopia
F. Uganda
G. Tanzania

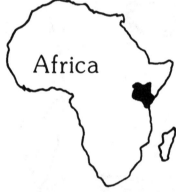

Africa

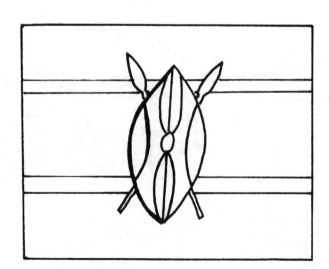

Kenya's national flag represents a Masai shield with two crossed spears meaning "defense of freedom." The top black stripe represents the Kenyan people; the middle red stripe stands for the blood shed for freedom and the lower green stripe symbolizes the rich land.

The two thin white stripes between the larger ones represent peace and unity.

GA1326

Birthdays

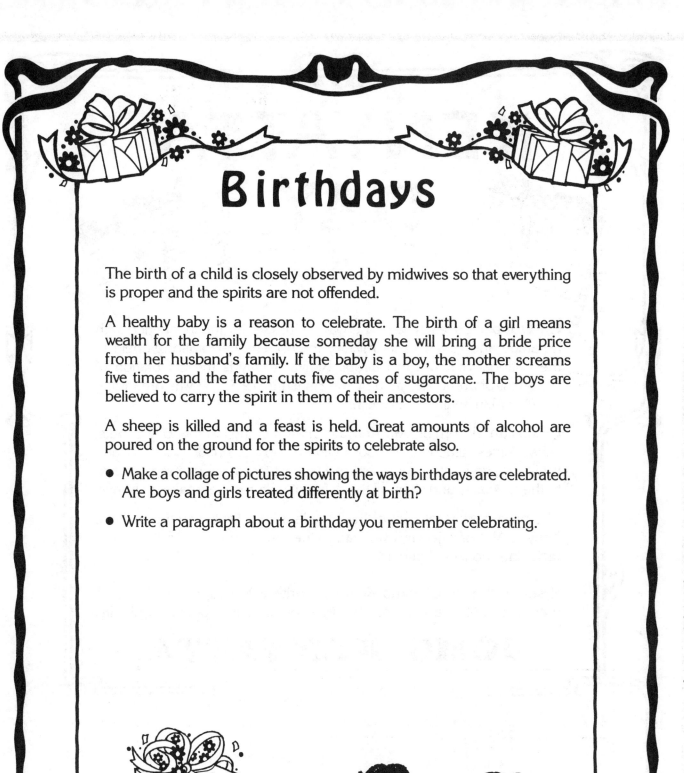

The birth of a child is closely observed by midwives so that everything is proper and the spirits are not offended.

A healthy baby is a reason to celebrate. The birth of a girl means wealth for the family because someday she will bring a bride price from her husband's family. If the baby is a boy, the mother screams five times and the father cuts five canes of sugarcane. The boys are believed to carry the spirit in them of their ancestors.

A sheep is killed and a feast is held. Great amounts of alcohol are poured on the ground for the spirits to celebrate also.

- Make a collage of pictures showing the ways birthdays are celebrated. Are boys and girls treated differently at birth?

- Write a paragraph about a birthday you remember celebrating.

GA1326

KENYATTA DAY

On October 25 each year, Kenya celebrates its independence with a parade and review of its military forces. The celebration is held in the National Stadium in Nairobi. Kenyatta Day is the celebration of the arrest of Jomo Kenyatta by the British in 1952. He was organizing the Mau Mau against the British.

Groups travel from all over Kenya to march in the parade. Boy Scouts, Girls Guides, teachers, school children, police, prison wardens and wildlife rangers are all represented. Dancers from different regions add to the spectacle and show all the different cultures that make up Kenya.

The most important part of the parade is the display by the military. Kenya's Air Force jets fly overhead as the army marches in full uniform, including monkey-skin hats.

Research the life of Jomo Kenyatta. Write a biography of his life. A time line could be used to visually show the high points in his life.

JOMO KENYATTA

GA1326

Dancing in Kenya

Dance is considered a very important form of expression in Kenya. Dances usually have a religious meaning. Young women may dance to ask the spirits to give them many healthy children.

A farming village may perform a special dance before planting new crops. They ask the spirits for a bountiful harvest.

The costumes worn during these dances may be very elaborate headdresses and masks. They may be decorated with feathers and painted very bright colors. Many look like birds, animals or fish.

- Design a mask out of papier-mâché, cardboard or heavy paper. Add feathers and paint details with fluorescent paint.

- Make a costume for yourself, a classmate or a doll. Research the different ethnic costumes worn by the regional tribes of Kenya.

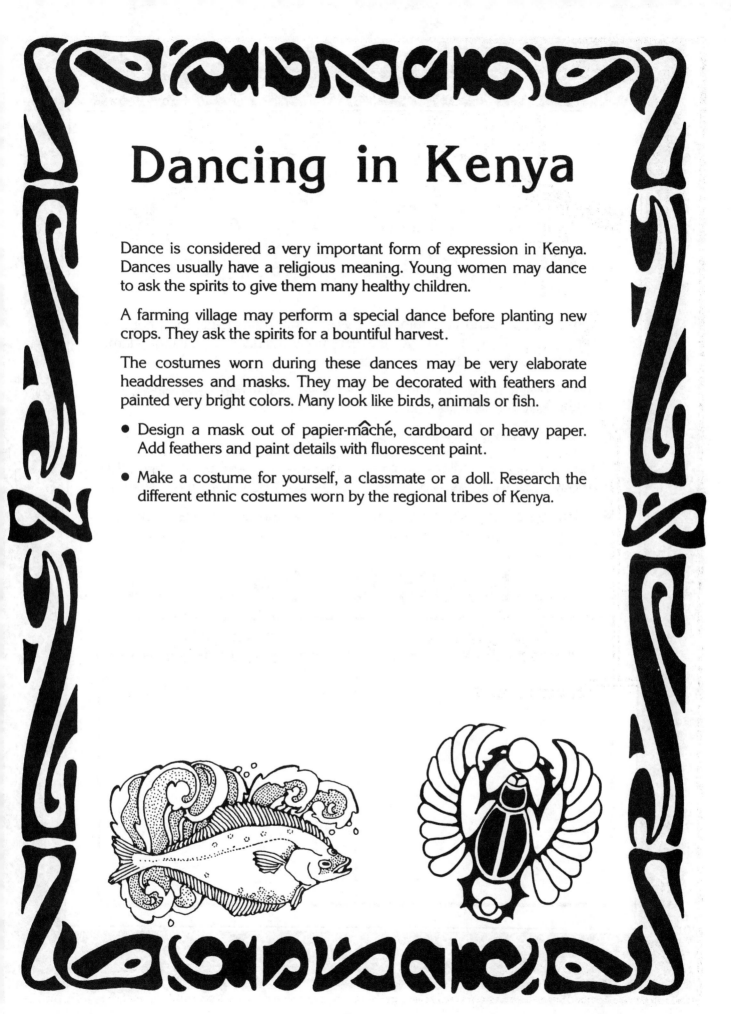

GA1326

When there has been little rain, the diviner (holy man) leads the people in a ceremony. If they are Kikuyu, the ceremony includes sacrificing a lamb while everyone faces Mt. Kenya and prays.

Jomo Kenyatta once wrote that he had seen many rain ceremonies, and "they are very soon followed by rain."

Do these ceremonies really work? Sometimes!

Often the American Indians would also have a rain ceremony. Research that cermony. How were the two ceremonies similar? How were they different?

- Try doing a puppet show demonstrating the rain ceremonies. Videotape the show to view by another class.

RAIN RITUAL

Native Kenyan	Native Indian

GA1326

Marriage Ceremonies

In prior years, a man could have more than one wife (polygamy). This was accepted by most Kenyans. Each wife had a separate hut, and all wives were treated equally. Today, supporting more than one wife is too expensive, and it is no longer an accepted practice.

When a man finds a woman he wants for a wife, he negotiates with her father. It is the custom for the girl to refuse the marriage four times and then the negotiations begin. A price is arranged before the marriage. The price can be an amount of money or a prearranged number of cattle.

The marriage is celebrated with a feast given at the husband's home.

- In the boxes below, list the pro and con arguments of the practice of polygamy. Then debate the issue, having the boys take the bride's side and the girls take the groom's side.

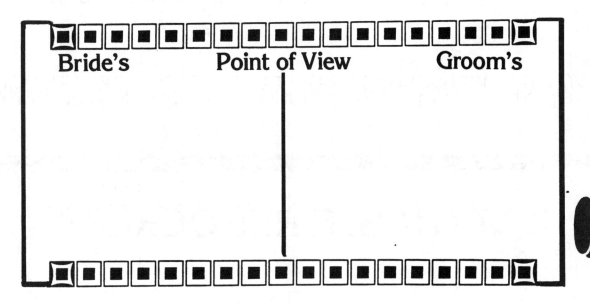

Bride's   Point of View   Groom's

Necklaces

Make necklaces similar to the ones worn in many ceremonies in Kenya. Use colored, plastic-covered wire. Cut one piece 18″ (45.7 cm) long for the main necklace. Add shorter pieces, curl, bend and twist them. Attach them to the main wire. Carefully try on your creation.

KENYA

ZIPPIN' ON...

- Find out more about the East African Safari Rally. This is Kenya's national auto race.

- Locate more information about animal safaris.

- Research the drums that are used in many of the ethnic ceremonies.

- Learn more about the Masai customs and culture.

VALUABLE RESOURCES

Khalfan, Z. M., and M. Amin. *We Live in Kenya*. New York: Bookright Press, 1984.

Lerner, H. *Kenya in Pictures*. Minneapolis: Lerner Publications, 1988.

Stein, R. C. *Enchantment of the World—Kenya*. Chicago: Children's Press, 1985.

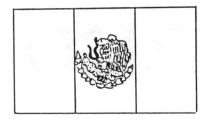
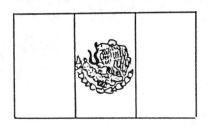
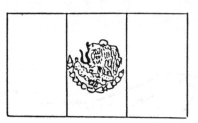

MEXICO

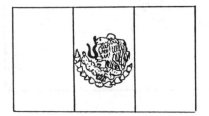
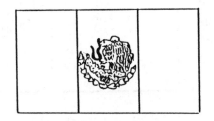
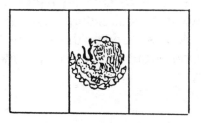

MEXICO

A. Gulf of Mexico
B. Pacific Ocean

1. Tijuana
2. Nogales
3. Monterrey
4. Guadalajara
5. Veracruz

6. Acapulco
7. Cancún
8. Puerto Vallarta
9. Mexico City*

The national flag of Mexico has three vertical stripes. From left to right they are green, which stands for independence; white, which stands for religion; and red, which stands for union. The center band contains Mexico's coat of arms. It represents an eagle with a snake in its beak sitting on cactus. This emblem is based on the ancient Aztec legend about the founding of Mexico City.

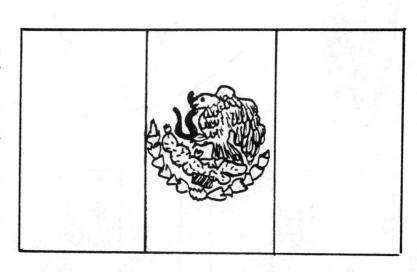

76

GA1326

CORPUS CHRISTI DAY

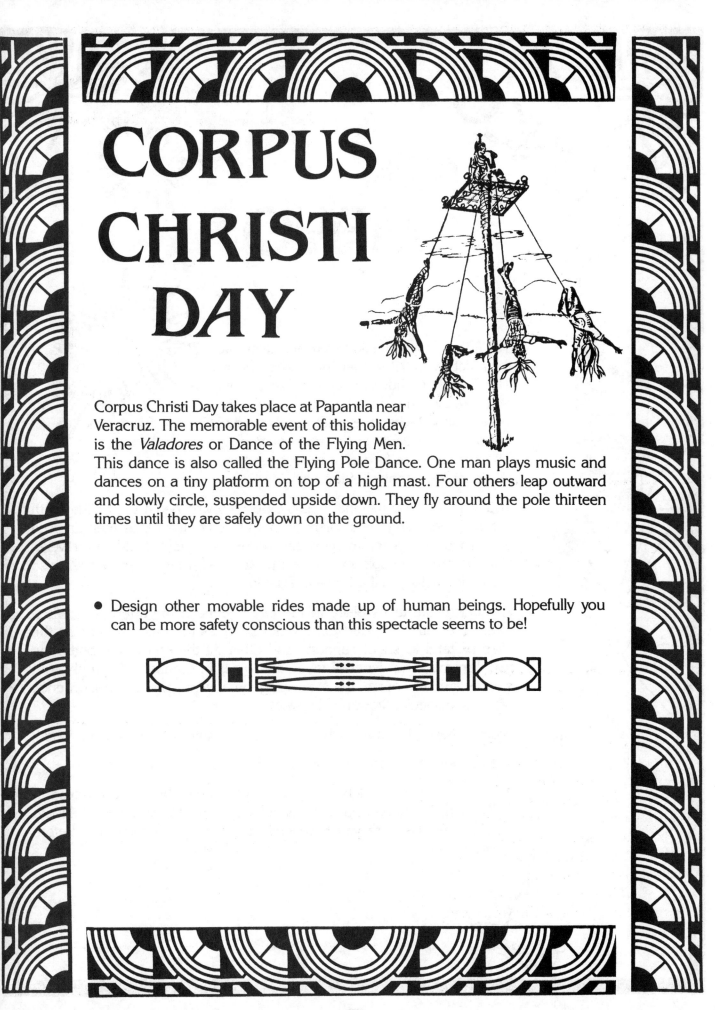

Corpus Christi Day takes place at Papantla near Veracruz. The memorable event of this holiday is the *Valadores* or Dance of the Flying Men. This dance is also called the Flying Pole Dance. One man plays music and dances on a tiny platform on top of a high mast. Four others leap outward and slowly circle, suspended upside down. They fly around the pole thirteen times until they are safely down on the ground.

- Design other movable rides made up of human beings. Hopefully you can be more safety conscious than this spectacle seems to be!

GA1326

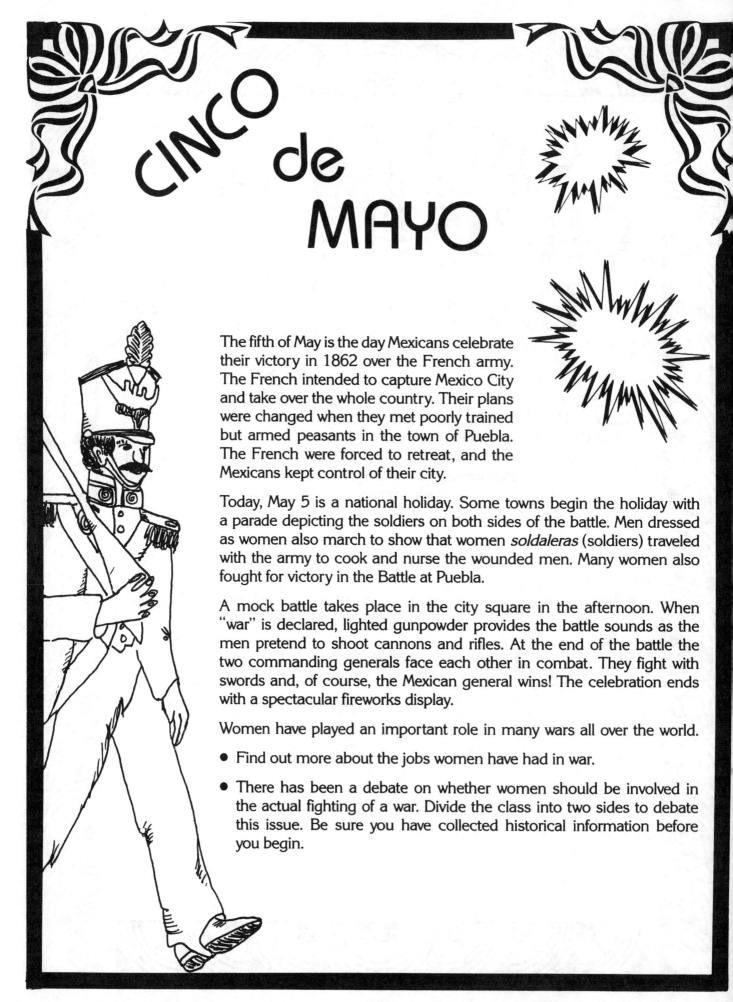

CINCO de MAYO

The fifth of May is the day Mexicans celebrate their victory in 1862 over the French army. The French intended to capture Mexico City and take over the whole country. Their plans were changed when they met poorly trained but armed peasants in the town of Puebla. The French were forced to retreat, and the Mexicans kept control of their city.

Today, May 5 is a national holiday. Some towns begin the holiday with a parade depicting the soldiers on both sides of the battle. Men dressed as women also march to show that women *soldaleras* (soldiers) traveled with the army to cook and nurse the wounded men. Many women also fought for victory in the Battle at Puebla.

A mock battle takes place in the city square in the afternoon. When "war" is declared, lighted gunpowder provides the battle sounds as the men pretend to shoot cannons and rifles. At the end of the battle the two commanding generals face each other in combat. They fight with swords and, of course, the Mexican general wins! The celebration ends with a spectacular fireworks display.

Women have played an important role in many wars all over the world.

- Find out more about the jobs women have had in war.

- There has been a debate on whether women should be involved in the actual fighting of a war. Divide the class into two sides to debate this issue. Be sure you have collected historical information before you begin.

GA1328

Independence Day

Independence Day is held September 16 and is a national holiday. The President of Mexico opens the ceremony by ringing Father Hidalgo's famous Liberty Bell in Mexico City.

In the evening, people gather in the central plazas of the towns to hear their mayors give what is called the *Grito de Dolores* (Cry of Dolores). Then the mayor starts a cry with "Mexicans, long live our heroes!" "Viva," the crowd shouts back. Then the mayor calls all heroes of the town by name.

At the end of the celebration, the mayor calls, "Viva, Mexico!" Then bands play the national anthem, church bells ring and fireworks explode.

Viva, Mexico!

- Write a folktale that tells why the mayor always gives the "Cry of Dolores."

Viva, Mexico!

GA1326

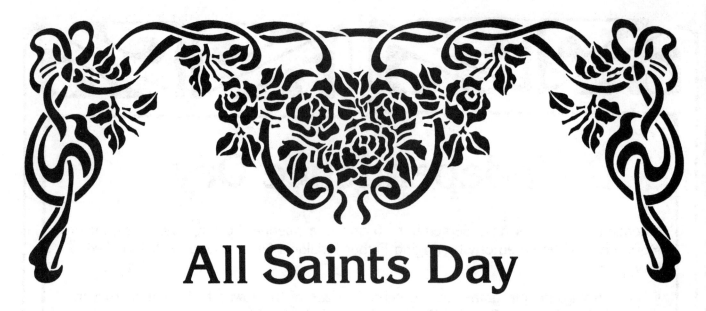

All Saints Day

All Saints Day is also known as the Day of the Dead. It is a feast day and not a sad affair. The families go to cemeteries and have parties. Food and drink are offered to the departed relatives as well as to the party-goers.

Bakers sell special "death bread" which is decorated with skulls of icing and sugar coffins. These breads are eaten in large quantities among the graves.

All Saints Day is a day to celebrate with the *spirit* of a dead friend or relative.

- If possible, go to a nearby cemetery and do one tombstone rubbing. If it is not possible to do a rubbing, sketch what you think the person looked like in the frame below. Try to find out more about the family or the person.

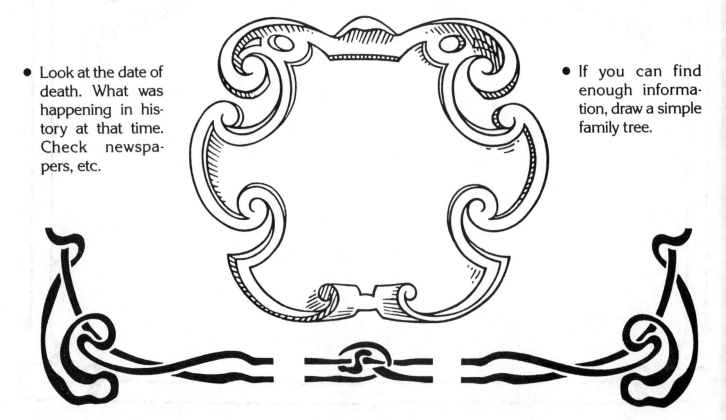

- Look at the date of death. What was happening in history at that time. Check newspapers, etc.

- If you can find enough information, draw a simple family tree.

GA1326

Christmas Posada

Christmas celebrations are extremely elaborate in Mexico. The nine days before Christmas are called the *posada*. Every night during the posada, families and friends join in the search for a refuge for the infant Jesus. The marchers are dressed in biblical costumes. They travel to a neighbor's home and ask for refuge. Every night except the last one they are turned away. On the last night they find refuge and a huge party is held.

One of the party highlights for children is the breaking of the *pinata*. Some are made of pottery; some are papier-mâché. Inside there are presents, pieces of candy, toys or other treasures. Some of the pinatas are shaped like animals, usually horses or dogs.

The children take turns trying to break the pinata with a long stick. When they succeed, there is a wild scramble to get the goodies.

- Besides hitting a pinata, what other way could children be involved in a game during the posada party? Can you invent a game children would like to play in someone's home or backyard?

- Do a pantomime of the pinata breaking. Do not use any props.

GA1326

GUADALUPE DAY

Guadalupe Day is celebrated on December 12. The legend behind this holiday began in 1531. It is said that the Virgin of Guadalupe appeared to a peasant named Juan Diego. She asked him to build a church in her honor. He was to convince the priests of her wishes. Also Juan should go into the hills and pick all of the roses he could find there. Now it was the dry season, so he should not have found any. But to Juan's surprise, he found the most beautiful roses he had ever seen. He put them inside his large cotton shirt to carry home. When he returned to his home, he took the roses out as he was telling the priests his story. When all the roses were removed, everyone saw the image of the Virgin printed on the shirt he had worn.

After seeing this miracle, a church was built in the Virgin of Guadalupe's honor. It is said to be built on the very spot where the Virgin spoke to Juan. Today the Virgin of Guadalupe is considered the Patron of the Republic.

Today on December 12, pilgrims travel to Guadalupe to visit the church. They often walk many days to get there. Often they will have their pictures taken in front of a mural depicting the Virgin's story.

Below write a letter to Juan Diego. Decide first of all if you believe his story or not. Tell him how you feel about the legend. Ask him questions.

GA1326

San Miguel Day takes place in San Miguel de Allende. The festival commemorates the feast day of St. Michael (Miguel), the patron saint of the town. It is said every Mexican named Miguel must come to this fiesta. It is very crowded!

Before dawn, people flock to the city plaza to "wake up Miguel." Dozens of mariachi bands all play at the same time. Fireworks go off. Bells in every church belfry ring. People make lots of noise.

At 10:00 a huge trailer truck opens and down a ramp come four or five giant black bulls. In the streets are several hundred young men and a few women. They are showing how brave they are. A few hold capes and try to fight the bulls like *matadors* at a bullfight. When the bulls are exhausted, they are loaded onto a truck.

Then a long parade starts. The *charros* (horsemen) and *charras* (horsewomen) lead the parade. Indian dancers, in full costume, dance in the parade.

In the evening fireworks are strung on tall poles and look like spiderwebs. The poles look like castle towers and are called castillos (castles). Pinwheels of fireworks are attached. Singing and dancing continue throughout the night.

Finally at about 4:00 a.m., the crowds begin to return home.

- Make a picture time line to depict the activities that take place during that twenty-four-hour time period.

- Design a float depicting this whole holiday.

- Make a fireworks display on black paper. Use different colors of glitter to show the *castillos*.

san miguel day

GA1326

MEXICO

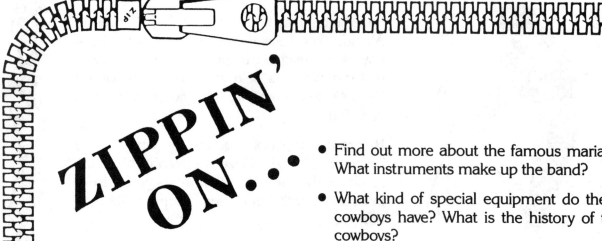

ZIPPIN' ON...

- Find out more about the famous mariachi band. What instruments make up the band?

- What kind of special equipment do the Mexican cowboys have? What is the history of these first cowboys?

- Research more about the Mayan civilization.

- How do you play jai alai, the fastest ball game in the world?

- What happens during the Mexican Mardi Gras?

- Columbus Day is also celebrated in almost every town. Why?

VALUABLE RESOURCES

Geography Department. *Mexico in Pictures*. Minneapolis: Lerner Publications, 1987.

Howard, J. *Mexico—The Land and Its People*. Morristown, NJ: Silver Burdett, 1986.

Irizarry, C. *Passport to Mexico*. New York: Franklin Watts, 1987.

Mexican Government Tourism Office. New York.

Somonte, C. *We Live in Mexico*. New York: Bookright Press, 1984.

GA1326

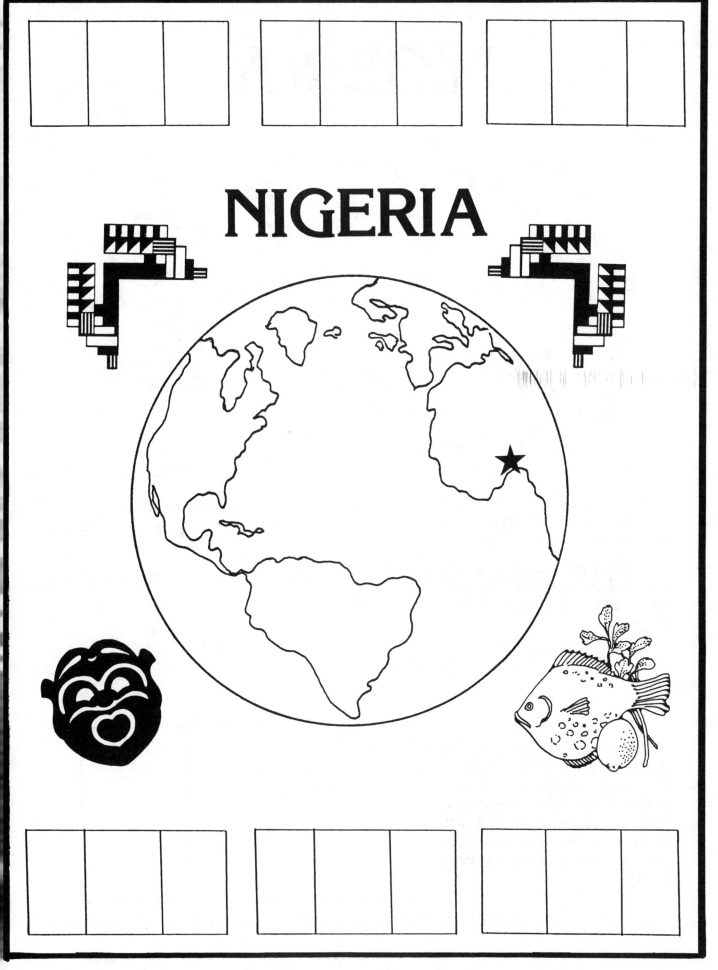

NIGERIA

GA1326

NIGERIA

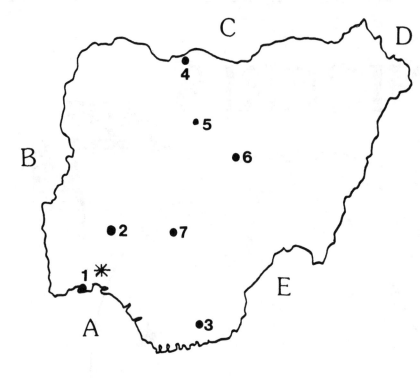

1. Lagos*
2. Oyo
3. Aba
4. Katsina
5. Zaria
6. Jos
7. Lokoja

A. Gulf of Guinea
B. Benin
C. Niger
D. Lake Chad
E. Cameroon

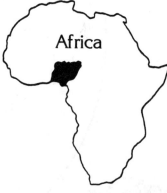

Africa

More Africans live in Nigeria than in any other country in Africa.

There are about 250 tribal groups with most of the population belonging to the Hausa-Fulani, Yoruba and Ibo groups.

Nigeria's flag has three vertical stripes of green, white and green. The design was chosen in a competition held in 1959. The winning designer was so impressed with Nigeria's forests that he chose green as the predominant color in the flag.

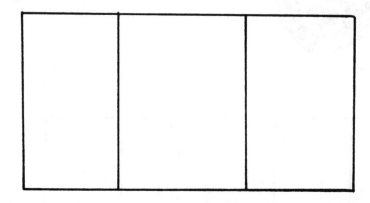

GA1326

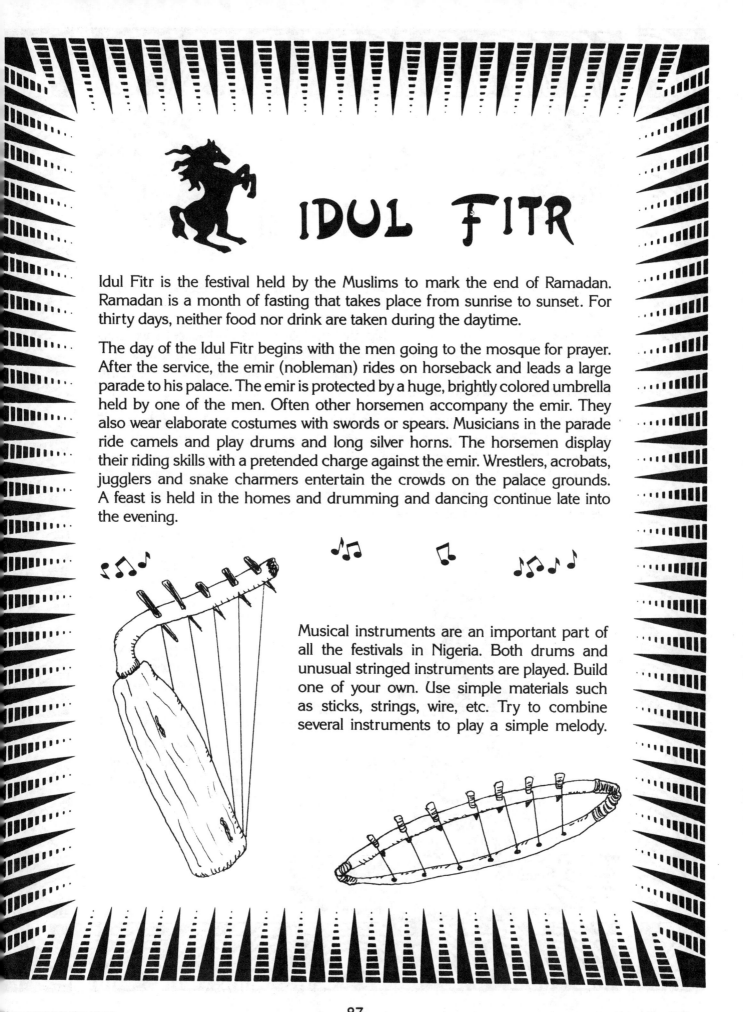

IDUL FITR

Idul Fitr is the festival held by the Muslims to mark the end of Ramadan. Ramadan is a month of fasting that takes place from sunrise to sunset. For thirty days, neither food nor drink are taken during the daytime.

The day of the Idul Fitr begins with the men going to the mosque for prayer. After the service, the emir (nobleman) rides on horseback and leads a large parade to his palace. The emir is protected by a huge, brightly colored umbrella held by one of the men. Often other horsemen accompany the emir. They also wear elaborate costumes with swords or spears. Musicians in the parade ride camels and play drums and long silver horns. The horsemen display their riding skills with a pretended charge against the emir. Wrestlers, acrobats, jugglers and snake charmers entertain the crowds on the palace grounds. A feast is held in the homes and drumming and dancing continue late into the evening.

Musical instruments are an important part of all the festivals in Nigeria. Both drums and unusual stringed instruments are played. Build one of your own. Use simple materials such as sticks, strings, wire, etc. Try to combine several instruments to play a simple melody.

87

GA1326

Epa Festival

The Yoruba people used to worship 420 gods and goddesses. Now only the main ones have celebrations.

The Epa Festival is held to worship the god of wood and also to worship the spirits of the ancestors. There are huge wooden masks worn during this celebration. The people believe the spirits of their ancestors will enter the masks while the men are dancing.

Master wood-carvers make the masks for the men to wear. The wood-carvers are called *Onishona* (people who make art). They also carve statues for the shrines of many of the worshipped gods and goddesses. It takes many hours to learn how to be a wood-carver. It can only be done by men. Other jobs that can only be done by men are carpentering, blacksmithing and cobblering. Weaving and pottery making are only done by women.

- Dancers wear huge carved displays of their ancestors' spirits on top of headdresses. Make a headdress using a box. Cut a hole in the box to fit your head; add strings to tie it onto your head. Add figures to the top that are made of cardboard or paper to represent your ancestors.

African Tribal Mask

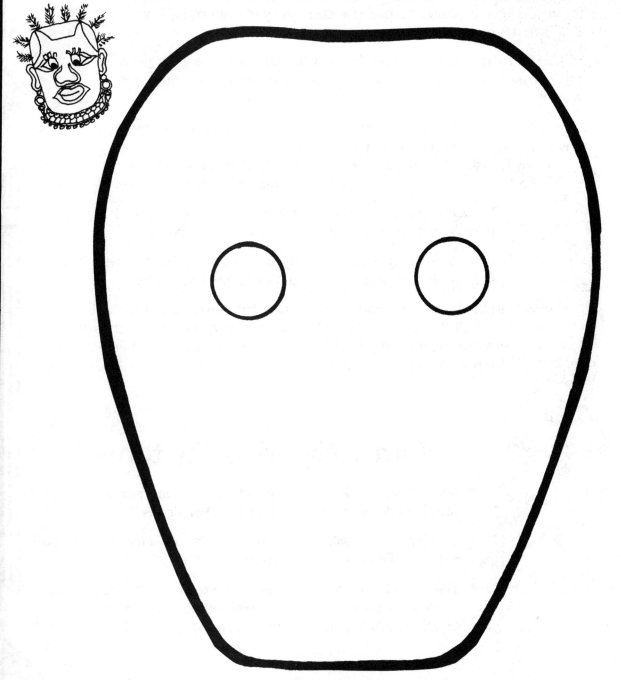

MATERIALS

1 6″ x 7″ (15.24 x 17.78 cm) piece of corrugated cardboard, feathers, construction paper, beads, cloth

Trace the basic mask shape onto brown corrugated cardboard. Cut out.

Glue feathers around the edge.

Make a large nose from cardboard or construction paper. Glue on.

Make large lips, eyelashes, eyebrows and ears from construction paper.

Add long earrings and a collar of colorful cloth or a beaded, wide necklace.

GA1326

Marriage Ceremony

Young men of marrying age are tested for their manhood among the Fulani. The test includes merciless beatings using birch branches. If the young man shows no pain, he can marry the girl of his choice; if he fails, he can *never* marry.

The custom of paying parents for a wife still continues in Nigeria. Nowadays, however, it is usually a mere token to please the family ancestors.

The marriage ritual varies greatly. Usually the celebration lasts several days. The Western-style marriage ceremony has become very popular with many Christian Nigerians. There are many bridesmaids and flower girls. The bride wears a veil, and there is a traditional wedding cake.

The wedding is an occasion for feasting and dancing. The family's wealth is evident by the extravagance of the celebration.

In the Ibo tribal group, polygamy is encouraged by the wives. They get help with the housework and with raising the children.

In the home, the man is the master. His senior wife is the authority over all the others. She helps the young wives and teaches them how to bring up their children. Each of the wives has her own hut for herself and her children.

Other Nigerian Customs

- Special handshakes show friendship and brotherhood. These same handshakes are used by black Americans.

- Touching food with your left hand is considered very bad manners. Pointing is also forbidden.

- The birth of twins is worshipped by the Yorubas. The Ibos despise them and connect them with misfortune. The mother is made to suffer for bringing them into the world.

What marriage customs do you have in your community?
- cutting the cake
- throwing the bouquet
- throwing rice
- tying cans onto the car

Use your imagination. Why do you think these traditions were started in your community?

GA1326

Huge numbers of men climb down the riverbanks of the Sokoto River at Argungu. This place is fished only once a year when the Sultan of Sokoto presides over the great fishing competition.

The fishermen look like giant dragonflies scooping up fish in the huge, wing-shaped nets. These nets are stretched over bamboo poles to give them the winged look.

Thousands of spectators watch as the fishermen try to catch the largest fish. Money prizes are awarded.

Fishing Competition

- Do an on-the-spot news report of the contest. You are the eyewitness reporter. Give all of the details occurring. Be sure to interview the winner with the biggest fish! What kinds of questions will you ask?

GA1326

NIGERIA

ZIPPIN' ON...

- Find out about the board games and card games that are popular at the marketplaces.

- Look for information about the following organizations in Nigeria: Red Cross, Girl Guides, Boy Scouts and the Y.M.C.A.

- Find out about the festival that takes place at the Oshun River. Women visit Oshogbo once a year for a special holiday.

- Look more into the roles of both men and women in society. Are these roles changing?

VALUABLE RESOURCES

Barker, C. *A Family in Nigeria*. Minneapolis: Lerner Publications, 1988.

Lerner, H. *Nigeria in Pictures*. Minneapolis: Lerner Publications, 1988.

Synge, R. *Nigeria—The Land and Its People*. London: Macdonald Educational Limited, 1985.

GA1326

SOVIET UNION

GA1326

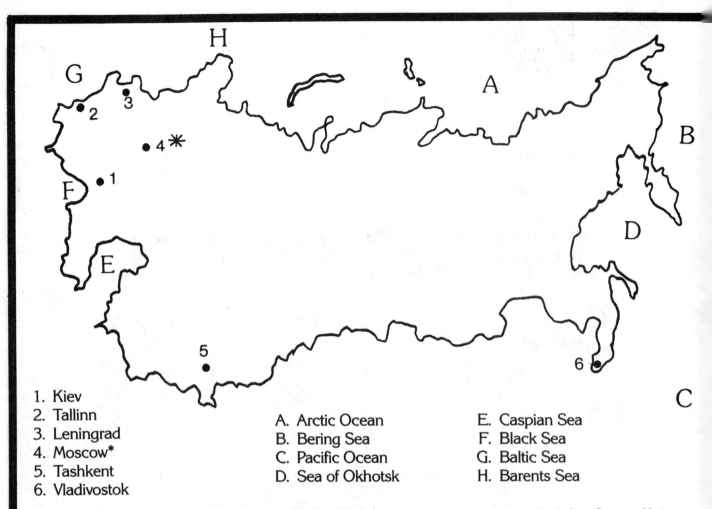

1. Kiev
2. Tallinn
3. Leningrad
4. Moscow*
5. Tashkent
6. Vladivostok

A. Arctic Ocean
B. Bering Sea
C. Pacific Ocean
D. Sea of Okhotsk

E. Caspian Sea
F. Black Sea
G. Baltic Sea
H. Barents Sea

The Union of Soviet Socialist Republics (U.S.S.R.) is sometimes also called the Soviet Union. It is the biggest country in the world and includes the two continents of Europe and Asia. Moscow is the capital.

There has been much unrest in the U.S.S.R. as many republics try to gain their independence.

SOVIET UNION

The flag of the Soviet Union is well-known all over the world. It is a plain red flag with a gold emblem in the upper-left corner. The emblem consists of a hammer crossed with a sickle. These symbolize industry and agriculture. The red star outlined in gold represents the Communist party.

The Easter religious holiday is considered the most important Christian holiday. An Easter church service is held in the famous Novodevichii Monastery in Moscow. The altar is covered in pure gold.

One way the Soviets celebrate this holiday is to prepare a special Easter cake, called a *koulich*. It is baked by the women and blessed by the church priests. It is a white cake with raisins, nuts and candied fruits. It is baked in a pan shaped like a stovepipe. The frosting often has the letters *KV* etched on it. *KV* stands for *Khristos voskress*, which means "Christ Is Risen."

Easter eggs are an important part of the celebration. They are boiled, dyed and decorated to adorn the Easter table.

The Easter meal begins with vodka and zakuska (appetizers) and ends with the Easter cake. There are also cold ham baked in rye dough, spicy sausages, cold baked ducks, cold suckling pig and Easter eggs.

EASTER

Koulich
(Easter Cake)

1 pkg. white cake mix with the ingredients listed on the package
⅓ cup (80 ml) raisins
½ cup (125 ml) chopped candied fruit
2-lb. (.9 g) coffee can, well-greased
3 T. (45 ml) chopped walnuts
½ tsp. (2.5 ml) vanilla
Basic recipe and ingredients for white icing
Sprinkles for decorating: sugared confetti, candied fruit, silver balls

Prepare the cake mix according to the package. Add raisins, fruit, nuts and vanilla.

Pour batter into a well-greased coffee can.

Bake at 350⁰ F (177⁰ C) for one hour. Cool cake; carefully remove it from the can. Spread icing on top and decorate with sprinkles. ENJOY!

GA1326

EGGS

Easter eggs have long been an important part of the Soviet Union's Easter celebration. Even before Christianity, eggs were considered symbols of the rebirth of nature.

Design either a Ukrainian or Fabergé egg below.

UKRAINIAN

FABERGÉ

The Ukrainians are famous for their decorated Easter eggs called *pysanky*. These eggs are not cooked or blown out. They are left uncovered and eventually dry out. These miniature mosaics have symbols that represent many things. Waves and ribbons mean life without end. Fish, crosses and triangles represent God. These symbols are drawn on with wax and then dipped in dye.

Decorated eggs are given as Easter gifts. Fabergé eggs are the most prized. They were made by Karl Fabergé who was the czar's jeweler. He created scenes with gold and precious stones. His eggs today are collected as art treasures.

96

GA1320

Russian Winter Festival

The Russian Winter Festival is celebrated for twelve days between December 25 and January 5. The festival has some similarity to Christmas, although Christmas is not officially recognized.

Evergreen trees are sold and decorated. They are called New Year's trees.

Grandfather Frost, *Dyed Maroz*, looks like Santa Claus. He wears a red suit and white beard.

Christmas cards are not exchanged because no cards are printed.

New Year's Day is the most important day during the festival. Carnivals, sports and special performances of the circus are performed. Toys are given to children by Grandfather Frost on this day along with spicy ginger cakes.

Matryoshka dolls are a traditional gift. They are unique in that they can be opened to reveal several smaller dolls nested inside each other.

Design your own *Matryoshka* dolls that represent Grandfather Frost. You may want to use your design on different sizes of empty, nested tin cans. They could be used to hold sprigs of evergreen, candies or small gifts.

GA1326

The MOSCO CIRCUS

The Russian Circus is an important event. There are special training schools for the acrobats, clowns and other performers. There are very high standards for these performers.

Find out more about the Clown College in Florida.

Practice a clown skit alone or with a group. Design your own clown faces and prepare costumes and props. Have a Clown Contest for another class. They can vote on the funniest act.

Great Soviet Composers

Some of the great Soviet composers wrote music for the ballet. Peter Tchaikovsky (1840-1893) wrote six symphonies including the *1812 Overture*. He wrote the music for the famous ballets *Swan Lake* and *The Nutcracker Suite*.

The Bolshoi Ballet is internationally known for its talented performers.

Sergei Prokofiev is another great musician who wrote the musical fairy tale of *Peter and the Wolf*.

Listen to the music of Tchaikovsky, Korsakov, Rachmaninoff and Prokofiev.

Create a watercolor painting of what you feel is happening in the music while listening to one of these famous masterpieces.

GA1326

Great October Revolution Day

Great October Revolution Day is celebrated on November 7. The November date is unusual but can be attributed to the fact that different countries long ago did not always follow the same calendar. The Soviet Union now uses the Gregorian calendar, as does most of the world. In early history, the Russian czars used the Julian calendar.

The Great October Revolution Day is a national celebration, but most of the major events take place in Moscow's Red Square and in Leningrad. May Day is celebrated on May 1 and is similar to the Great October Revolution Day. Buildings and streets are decorated with bunting, streamers and flags. There are many parades with bands, soldiers, tanks, gymnasts, dance groups, children carrying red flags, farm workers and factory workers. The parade lasts all day and may even go on into the night. It ends with a huge display of fireworks.

One of the most familiar sites in Moscow's Red Square is St. Basil's Cathedral. Its towers and onion-shaped domes are painted in red, yellow, blue, green and gold designs. The architect of St. Basil's was blinded by Ivan the Terrible so he could never again build anything of such great beauty.

Try making a picture of St. Basil's Cathedral using baker's clay. Looking at the picture below, or one in color, press the basic building shapes out of clay. Add details to the onion domes, etc. After baking, paint with many colors and add gold paint for accents.

Red Square

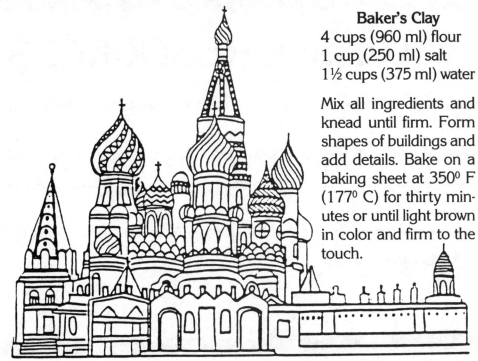

May Day

Baker's Clay
4 cups (960 ml) flour
1 cup (250 ml) salt
1½ cups (375 ml) water

Mix all ingredients and knead until firm. Form shapes of buildings and add details. Bake on a baking sheet at 350° F (177° C) for thirty minutes or until light brown in color and firm to the touch.

GA1326

SOVIET UNION

ZIPPIN' ON...

- Learn about the May Day celebration.

- Weddings take place in a government building. How are they different from the wedding ceremonies and parties you have gone to?

- New Year's trees are decorated evergreen trees. What kind of ornaments are used?

- Read the fairy tale of Baba Yaga. Is it similar to a tale you have heard before?

- Find out about the Children's Railroad. The best-known one is in Kiev.

- Learn a Cossack dance. Wear the familiar costume and perform for your class.

VALUABLE RESOURCES

Gantz, D. *Let's Visit the Soviet Union—A Passport Sticker Book.* New York: Simon & Schuster, Inc., 1989.

Gillies, J. *The Soviet Union—The World's Largest Country.* Minneapolis: Dillion Press, 1985.

Lewis, L., and M. Tolhurst. *People and Places—U.S.S.R.* Morristown, NJ: Silver Burdett, 1988.

Riordan, J. *Soviet Union—The Land and Its People.* Morristown, NJ: Silver Burdett, 1986.

U.S.S.R. (Intourist). New York.

GA1326

SPAIN

GA1326

SPAIN

1. Madrid*
2. Barcelona
3. Valencia
4. Alicante
5. Granada
6. Córdoba
7. Seville
8. San Sebastián

A. Bay of Biscay
B. Mediterranean Sea
C. Strait of Gibraltar
D. Portugal

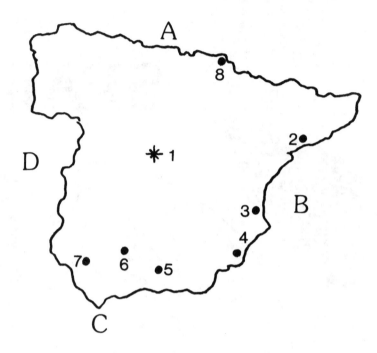

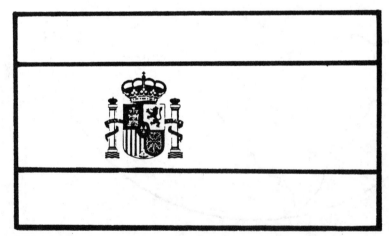

The present-day flag of Spain uses the striped red and yellow colors from the twelfth century kingdom of Aragon.

The center yellow stripe is twice as wide as each of the red stripes.

This present-day flag, used by the government, was adopted in 1981.

The flag is shown with only the horizontal stripes or with the national coat of arms on the left side.

GA1326

FESTIVAL OF FOOLS

On December 28, the Day of the Holy Innocents or Fool's Festival, men with white faces (usually covered with a white mask), choose a mayor. He assumes the city's authority for the day. The group of men, dressed as clowns or women, go to the local banks and shops and give out fines. In the evening, these masked figures appear again and read a list of complaints criticizing the local people and their places of business. All of this is done in fun. A similar celebration is held at Christmastime in Alicante and is called Fool's Festival.

You may want to impose fines in school on teachers, principal, secretary, custodian, lunchroom helpers, etc.

Be sure it is done in fun!

Design a clever form to hand out when a fine is imposed.

Mayos

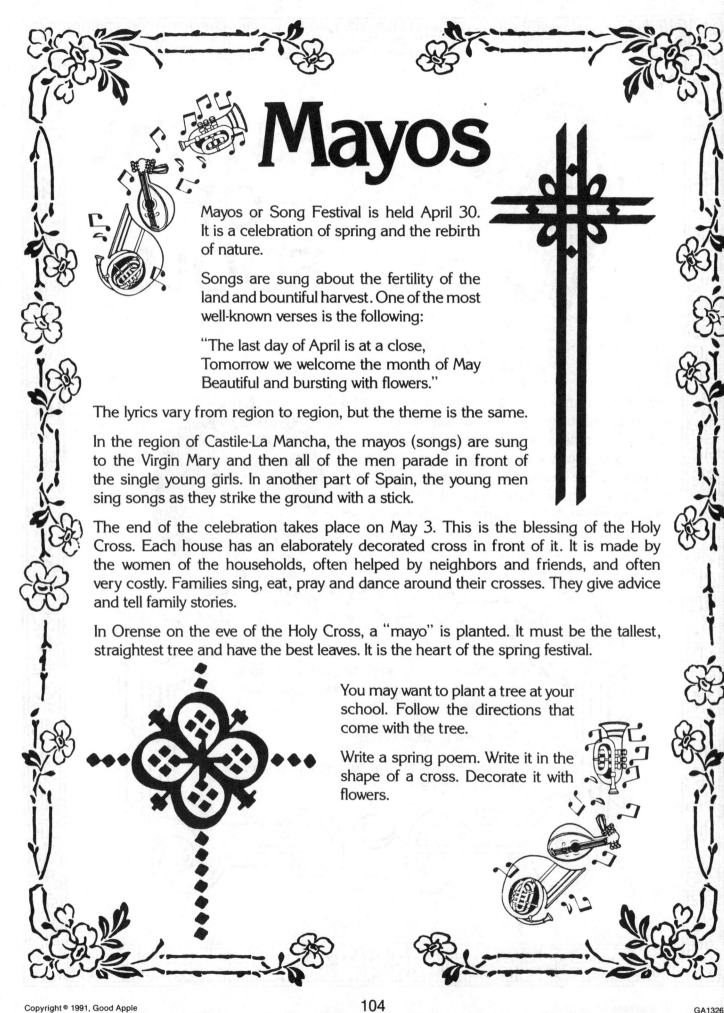

Mayos or Song Festival is held April 30. It is a celebration of spring and the rebirth of nature.

Songs are sung about the fertility of the land and bountiful harvest. One of the most well-known verses is the following:

"The last day of April is at a close,
Tomorrow we welcome the month of May
Beautiful and bursting with flowers."

The lyrics vary from region to region, but the theme is the same.

In the region of Castile-La Mancha, the mayos (songs) are sung to the Virgin Mary and then all of the men parade in front of the single young girls. In another part of Spain, the young men sing songs as they strike the ground with a stick.

The end of the celebration takes place on May 3. This is the blessing of the Holy Cross. Each house has an elaborately decorated cross in front of it. It is made by the women of the households, often helped by neighbors and friends, and often very costly. Families sing, eat, pray and dance around their crosses. They give advice and tell family stories.

In Orense on the eve of the Holy Cross, a "mayo" is planted. It must be the tallest, straightest tree and have the best leaves. It is the heart of the spring festival.

You may want to plant a tree at your school. Follow the directions that come with the tree.

Write a spring poem. Write it in the shape of a cross. Decorate it with flowers.

SEMANA SANTA

One of the most impressive festivals is Semana Santa or Holy Week. Throughout Spain it is a time of devotion and pageantry. The city of Seville comes to a halt for this celebration. Weeks before, elaborate statues that represent the events of the final days in Christ's life are made. These statues are carried in a procession to the cathedral. Some of the statues have moving parts. These are a favorite of the crowds. These elaborate "floats" weigh up to a thousand pounds and are carried by processioners. Because of the enormous weight, the men are formed into teams for specific time allotments. The statue carriers march to the rhythm of trumpets and drums.

Each cathedral has a men's organization known as a brotherhood. They raise money throughout the year to sponsor the events they are in charge of during Holy Week. They march as a group in the parade often wearing pointed hats that also cover their faces. Each carries a long stick which has a candle holder on the top for night parades.

In Aragon, a tin drum is beaten by hand. The harder the drum is beaten, even if bloody hands occur, is a sign that the drummer's duty has been fulfilled. The roll of the drum signals the start of the period of mourning for Christ. In Cordoba there is a fierce competition to see who can drum the fastest.

In Murcia, a parade is held by the brotherhoods. There is a competition for the most elaborate floats, costumes and beautifully decorated horses.

Holy Week is a solemn occasion, yet it has a parade. Why? Why is there music? Why are there costumes?

What expressions of sadness would you see at a funeral in your town?

Is there a parade, music, special clothing worn?

Holy Week

GA1326

CHRISTMAS

Christmas is celebrated to commemorate the birth of Christ. December 25 was chosen, it is thought, to combat the pagan sun festival held the same day.

Carols are sung outdoors where various groups of hand bell ringers and carol singers are accompanied by musicians playing mandolins, tambourines and guitars.

On Christmas Eve, called Night of Good Tidings, the midnight mass is held. It ends before midnight because it is believed the cock crowed for the first time at midnight, then at three and six o'clock.

One of the most unusual Christmas celebrations centers around Olentzero. He is a charcoal burner who comes down the mountains into town to tell the good news of Christ's birth. In several towns on Christmas Eve, this reenactment also includes carrying Olentzero through town high on the shoulders of many different groups of men. This tradition died out after Spain's civil war but has reappeared and changed slightly since the 1960's.

Nativity scenes and plays are given all over Spain. One of the well-known performances takes place in Barcelona.

Another Christmas custom that takes place in Catalonia is a lucky strike game. A tree trunk is filled with sweets and presents. Children hit at the trunk trying to knock out the hazel nuts, almonds, toffee and other goodies.

Spain has the legendary figure Olentzero, a coal miner who announces Christ's birth. Who or what do other cultures use to bring the news to the people?

EPIPHANY

GA1326

Festival
of
San Fermin

The Festival of San Fermin is held between July 7 and 14. Each morning a rocket is fired from the town hall and that signals the start of the running of the bulls. About a dozen bulls are released from a pen and race along a route of about a half mile to where the bullring is. Close to 1000 young men run ahead of the bulls and dodge their horns. Thousands of spectators watch this feat of daring. Tourists also are allowed to run in the event. Street merchants sell red berets, sashes and neckerchiefs. Participants must follow strict rules about clothing and behavior. They must be careful not to wear unusual costumes or make gestures that would single them out and catch the bull's attention.

Draw a comic strip of the running of the bulls from the bull's point of view.

title

			the end

GA1326

FESTIVAL of FIRE

In Valencia, the Festival of Fire is celebrated for a week. The city, in mid-March, has more than three hundred town squares decorated with giant sculptures. These statues are called *falla* meaning "fire." A typical sculpture will have two or three large figures displayed in a scene depicting a humorous, modern event. The fallas are similar to a nonmovable parade float. Some fallas take a year to build and are so large they do not fit in the narrow streets. They have to be lifted into place by large cranes. A few of the statues are kept and placed in a museum, but the majority go up in flames on the last night of the festival.

The origin of this festival is traced back to the annual burning of the wood scraps and rubbish supplied by the town carpenters.

The morning following the burning of the fallas shows little remnants left of the festival. The streets are scrubbed clean and the large number of artists and display specialists have already begun designing the next year's creations.

Design a humorous scene with several statues included. It could depict a newsworthy event in your school, city or state.

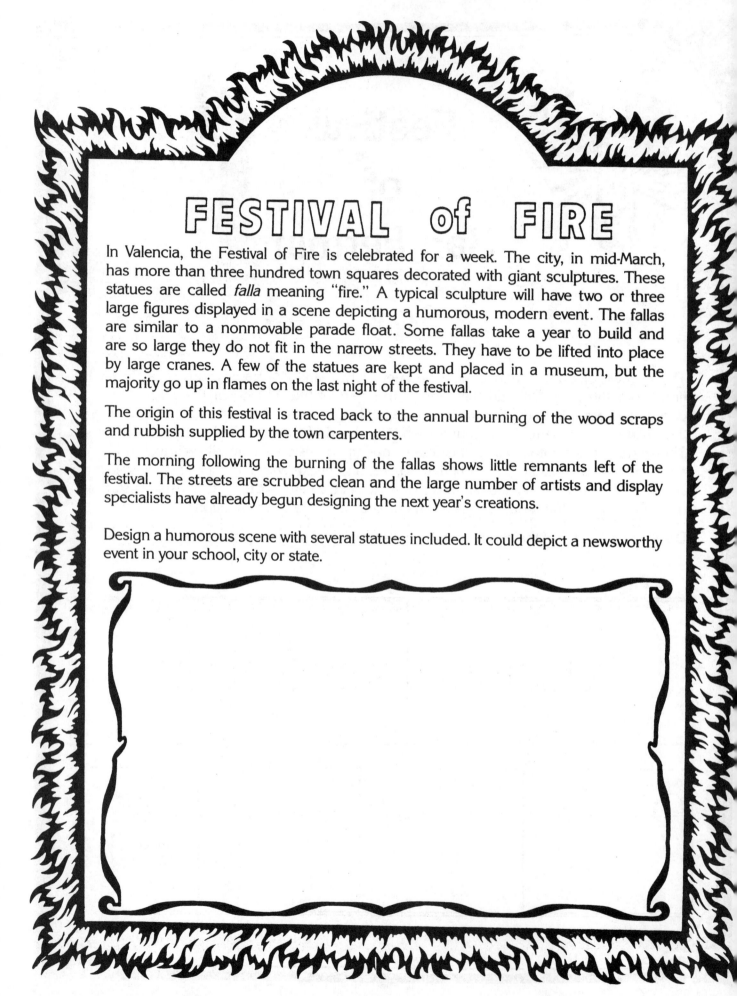

GA1326

SPAIN

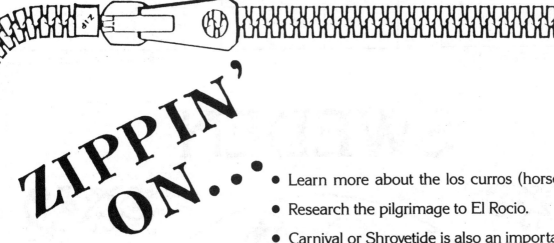

ZIPPIN' ON....

- Learn more about the los curros (horse corrals).
- Research the pilgrimage to El Rocio.
- Carnival or Shrovetide is also an important festival in Spain.
- San Sebastián or St. Stephen's Festival is celebrated in special ways in Spain.
- Children in Spain enjoy the pranks of the Little Bishop's Celebration. Learn more about it.

VALUABLE RESOURCES

Cross, E., and W. Cross. *Enchantment of the World—Spain*. Chicago: Children's Press, 1985.

Galford, E. *Spain*. Alexandria, VA: Time-Life Books, 1987.

Sanchez, M. *Celebrating in Spain*. Madrid, Spain: Secretary General of Tourism, 1990.

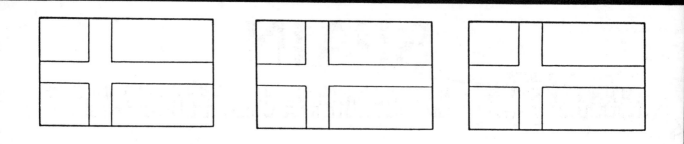

SWEDEN

110

SWEDEN

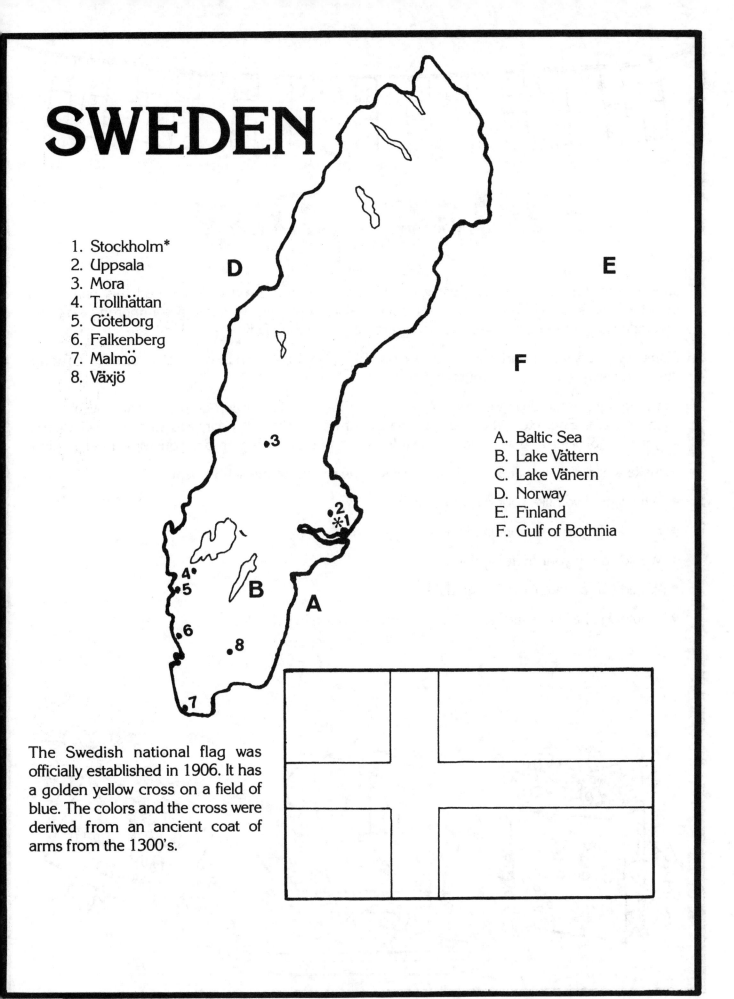

1. Stockholm*
2. Uppsala
3. Mora
4. Trollhättan
5. Göteborg
6. Falkenberg
7. Malmö
8. Växjö

A. Baltic Sea
B. Lake Vättern
C. Lake Vänern
D. Norway
E. Finland
F. Gulf of Bothnia

The Swedish national flag was officially established in 1906. It has a golden yellow cross on a field of blue. The colors and the cross were derived from an ancient coat of arms from the 1300's.

GA1326

Flag Day

June 6 has the name day of Gustav or Gustavus. Several Swedish kings had this name and thus the day is celebrated in the kings' honor. This event began nearly two hundred years ago and today is celebrated as Sweden's national birthday or Flag Day.

Flags are everywhere and parades are held. Because Sweden has been at peace for so long, this day seems to go without much notice.

Not long ago, name days were celebrated instead of birthdays. Each calendar date had a name, such as Sara, Eric, etc. When your name occurred on the calendar, you had a special party in your honor. Name days made it easy for your friends to remember you with a celebration.

- Make a name day calendar for your class for one month of the school year.

- What would you like your day to be like?

- How would you celebrate in school?

- Would you or your friends bring a treat?

- Would you be in charge for the day?

- Would you have to share your day with someone else in your class?

St. Lucia Day

Saint Lucia is a symbol of light and reminds the Swedish people that after December the long dark nights will get shorter.

The day was named after a young girl who, during Roman times, was put to death for her Christian beliefs.

St. Lucia Day is celebrated on December 13. Early in the morning, a young girl in each family is awakened, dressed in a white robe with a red ribbon around the waist and crowned with a circle of candles. Her duty is to bring breakfast to her family. Special sweet buns flavored with saffron are served. Boys, called star boys, wear long white shirts and pointed hats. They help carry the sweets.

The celebration has grown and now clubs and factories also select their own Lucias. Parades and parties are held as everyone gets ready for Christmas. Swedish school children, dressed as Lucia, bring morning coffee and cakes to their teachers.

- Design a greeting card that could be given on St. Lucia Day. It could also be a tag that was attached to a package with a sweet bun inside.

- Using the recipe, make sweet buns and celebrate St. Lucia Day.

INGREDIENTS

1 c. (250 ml) milk	5 grains saffron
2 oz. (59.15 ml) yeast (or 2 heaping T. [30 ml])	1 egg
	4 c. (960 ml) flour
6 oz. (177.44 ml) butter	¾ c. (180 ml) sugar
	25 almonds
1 c. (250 ml) raisins	

Garnish: 1 beaten egg, sugar and 10 chopped almonds.

Warm milk and saffron. Stir in yeast and bit of sugar. Add flour and egg. Mix until smooth. Stir sugar and butter until light and creamy; add to dough. Work in raisins. Let rise for thirty minutes. Scald almonds; chop fine; add to dough.

Place dough on floured board. Shape into buns. Place on buttered baking sheet. Let rise twenty minutes. Brush with garnish. Bake at 450⁰ F (232⁰ C) until golden brown. Serve warm.

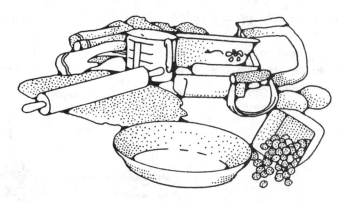

GA1326

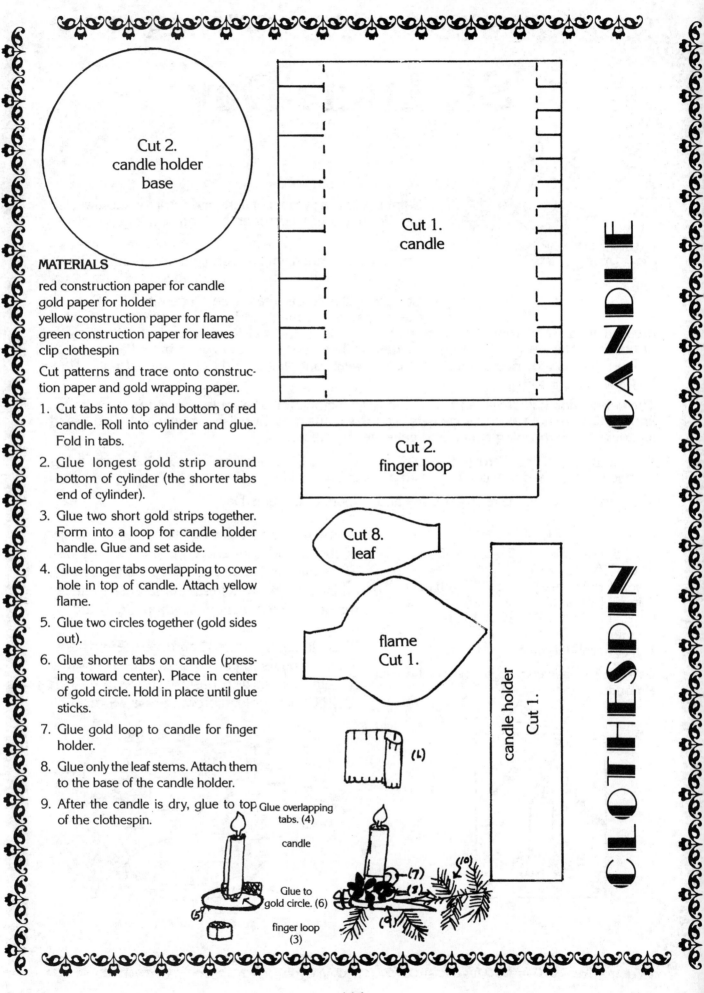

Cut 2.
candle holder
base

Cut 1.
candle

CANDLE

MATERIALS

red construction paper for candle
gold paper for holder
yellow construction paper for flame
green construction paper for leaves
clip clothespin

Cut patterns and trace onto construction paper and gold wrapping paper.

1. Cut tabs into top and bottom of red candle. Roll into cylinder and glue. Fold in tabs.

2. Glue longest gold strip around bottom of cylinder (the shorter tabs end of cylinder).

3. Glue two short gold strips together. Form into a loop for candle holder handle. Glue and set aside.

4. Glue longer tabs overlapping to cover hole in top of candle. Attach yellow flame.

5. Glue two circles together (gold sides out).

6. Glue shorter tabs on candle (pressing toward center). Place in center of gold circle. Hold in place until glue sticks.

7. Glue gold loop to candle for finger holder.

8. Glue only the leaf stems. Attach them to the base of the candle holder.

9. After the candle is dry, glue to top of the clothespin.

Cut 2.
finger loop

Cut 8.
leaf

flame
Cut 1.

candle holder
Cut 1.

CLOTHESPIN

(1)

Glue overlapping tabs. (4)

candle

Glue to gold circle. (6)

finger loop (3)

(5)

(7)

(8)

(10)

(9)

GA1326

Following St. Lucia Day on December 13, everyone starts Christmas preparations. The house is cleaned and gingerbread is made. Bundles of wheat are tied and placed outdoors for the birds. Holiday breads and cakes are baked. Candles are an important part of the Christmas celebration. They represent the desire for the return of light. On December 22, the darkest, shortest day, candles are placed in the churchyards too.

Christmas evergreen trees are decorated with old-fashioned straw ornaments. Straw goats are seen everywhere. They represent the old god Thor.

Presents are exchanged. Long ago funny gifts called *julklappar* were given by a secret rap on the door. Other presents were brought by Jul Tomten, the Christmas elf. The father of the household would put on a long beard and dress like Jul Tomten when he handed out the presents.

Special Christmas foods are eaten, too. *Lutefish*, dried cod, is boiled and eaten with melted butter. Sweets, also made especially for Christmas, are kringle, sandbakkels and krumkake.

Christmas cards are exchanged, too. Advent calendars are hung for children to open the twenty-four days before Christmas.

The celebration does not stop at Christmas but goes on to January 13—St. Knut's Day. New Year's is also celebrated with bells, parties and parades.

- Try making one of the Swedish Christmas sweets.
- Make a garland of Swedish flags for your tree.
- Read more about Tomten.

CHRISTMAS

GA1326

Tomten

A little gnome named Tomten is a good-natured elf with short legs, long beard and a red tasseled cap. He is seldom seen but can be coaxed to the house by a bowl of rice pudding placed on the doorstep.

Make a small Tomten using colored modeling clay.

 Basic body shape with buttons.

 Add legs with elf shoes.

  Press white clay through a garlic press to make strings for the beard and hair.

 Add a red cap with a tassel.

JULBROCK

Julbrock is the Swedish goat that Tomten rides. It is seen in many Christmas decorations. Usually the Julbrock is made of straw. It is made in many different sizes from 1 inch (2.54 cm) to 3 feet (.91 m).

Try making a Julbrock for your tree. Adjust the sizes to the size you need.

MATERIALS

tan yarn, red yarn or heavy string, 2 brown pipe cleaners (6″ [15.24 cm]), 2 squiggle eyes

Cut three bundles of yarn—ten 8″ (20.32 cm) pieces and two bundles of ten 6″ (15.24 cm) pieces. Lay the short bundle lengthwise. Tie 5″ (12.7 cm) red yarn around each, ½″ (1.25 cm) from end. This is the body of the horse. Tie the other two bundles ½″ (1.25 cm) and 1½″ (3.79 cm) from each end. These are the legs.

Place the body between the two legs and tie in place. Before tying the neck, place pipe cleaners into yarn. Curl pipe cleaners. Add squiggle eyes and red yarn for reins and black thread for a loop to hang on the tree.

Dalarna Horses

Dalarna horses are world famous. These horses are made of wood and whittled during long winter evenings. Most often painted red, they are decorated with bright colored flowers.

Fold an 8″ (20.32 cm) piece of cardboard or heavy red paper in half. Cut two patterns and glue so it can stand up. (If using cardboard, paint two coats of red on the shape.) Then add flowers for the saddle and harness. Use either painted, silk or paper flowers. Add gold paint for the reins. Paint, paper or yarn would be good for the mane and tail.

GA1326

Midsummer Festival

On the Saturday nearest June 24, the Swedes celebrate Midsummer. It is the longest day of the year. Midsummer was originally a pagan festival.

A tall pole is decorated with green leaves, streamers and flowers. It is never put up before Midsummer Eve. The maypole (majstang) is placed in a park or in the center of town. The townspeople dance, sing and play games around the pole. Music is played on violins and accordions. People stay up all night until sunrise— which is not a very long time on this day!

In Dalarna, ethnic customs are enjoyed. One of these customs is having the women take a traditional "church boat" to the Midsummer Festival service. They are dressed in traditional ethnic costumes and sing old hymns. Two fiddlers play as the pastor stands at the stern of the boat.

- Try making a maypole. Streamers of crepe paper could be attached to the top. Dance in two different directions weaving the streamers around the pole as you go. Select some music that you can do a lively dance to.

GA1326

SWEDEN

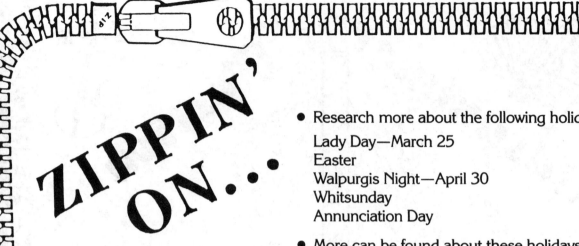

- Research more about the following holidays:

  Lady Day—March 25
  Easter
  Walpurgis Night—April 30
  Whitsunday
  Annunciation Day

- More can be found about these holidays also:

  Shrove Tuesday or Fat Tuesday, before Lent
  New Year celebration and Tennyson's poem,
    "Ring Out, Wild Bells"
  Crane Eve
  Crayfish Festival—August
  All Saint's Day—November 1
  Great Lapp Winter Fair

VALUABLE RESOURCES

Constable, G. *Scandinavia*. Amsterdam: Time-Life Books, 1985.

Hintz, M. *Enchantment of the World—Sweden*. Chicago: Children's Press, 1985.

Keeler, S., and C. Fairclough. *We Live in Sweden*. New York: Bookright Press, 1985.

Olsson, I. *Sweden—A Good Life for All*. Minneapolis: Dillon Press, 1983.

Orton, G. *Scandinavia*. Morristown, NJ: Silver Burdett, 1985.

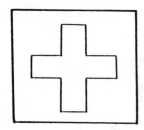 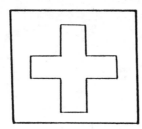 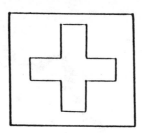 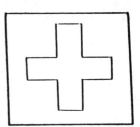

SWITZERLAND

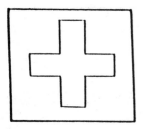 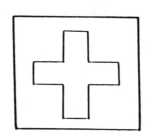 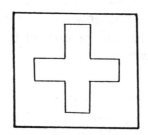 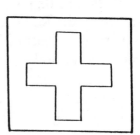

119

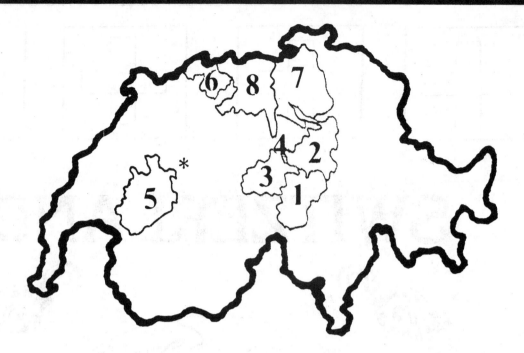

Bern*
1. Uri
2. Schwyz
3. Unterwalden
4. Lake Lucerne
5. Fribourg
6. Basel
7. Zurich
8. Aargau

SWITZERLAND

The official flag of Switzerland is square. A white cross lies on a field of red. The white cross, a sign of the holy cross, has been used in Switzerland since medieval times.

Draw one of the medieval flags that was a part of Switzerland at that time.

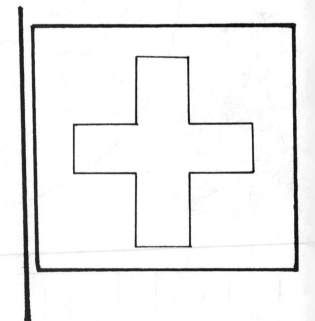

Switzerland's flag is very similar to the organization known as the Red Cross. Is this only a coincidence, or is there a reason? Try to find the answer to this. Record your findings below.

GA13

SWISS NATIONAL DAY

The arrival of August 1 heralds a national celebration commemorating the year 1291 when the cantons (states) of Uri, Schwyz and Unterwalden met and formed an alliance.

The day is now celebrated with speeches; singing of the national anthem, "Swiss Psalm"; music programs; folk dancing; parades with native costumes and a bonfire.

The streets and buildings are decorated with national, state and community flags. In wealthy communities, fireworks are displayed. Bell ringing and bonfires are part of the celebration. The bonfires in the mountains remind the Swiss of the days when fires were used to send messages between the isolated mountain towns.

Children parade through the streets in the evening, carrying lighted paper lanterns.

The Rhine Falls at Neuhausen are spectacularly lighted only on this special evening. Fireworks displays bring many spectators.

- Locate the three cantons that formed the alliance in 1291.
- Research the state, national and community flags. Design a flag for your community, school or class.
- Bake small cupcakes or rolls and make small flags to insert into them.
- Discuss the children's tradition of carrying paper lanterns. Would your community allow this parade if it were a custom?

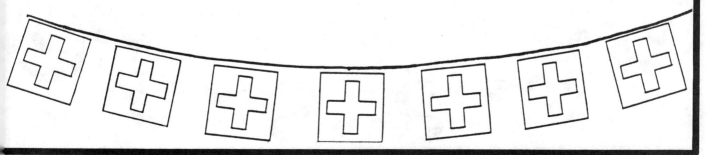

Klausjagen

The Christmas celebration in Switzerland begins with the "pursuit of St. Nicholas"—*Klausjagen*. On December 5 in the village of Küssnacht near Lake Lucerne, 200 or more marchers carry huge bishops' hats (6 ft. [1.82 m] tall) cut out of cardboard and decorated to look like lace patterns.

A lit candle is inside and carried over the heads of the marchers. These headdresses were originally worn only by men, but today both men and women are part of the parade. St. Nicholas is escorted through the town accompanied by the marchers.

Bells echo through the streets as strong men carry heavy bells around their necks. Horn blowing and brass bands add to the excitement.

Design a pattern in this bishop's hat.

At the head of the parade are the whip crackers who announce, with the cracking of their 5 to 8-foot (1.52 to 2.44 m) whips, the arrival of the procession.

On the evening of December 6 in the city of Fribourg, St. Nicholas rides through town on a donkey. When reaching the square, he gives a speech about the events of the past year. Everyone then goes to the school for a festive meal.

The legend of St. Nicholas tells of three children who were brought back to life after being killed by a butcher. St. Nicholas has become the patron saint to children—especially boys.

In the space below, write what you think the details are to the legend surrounding the three children and St. Nicholas.

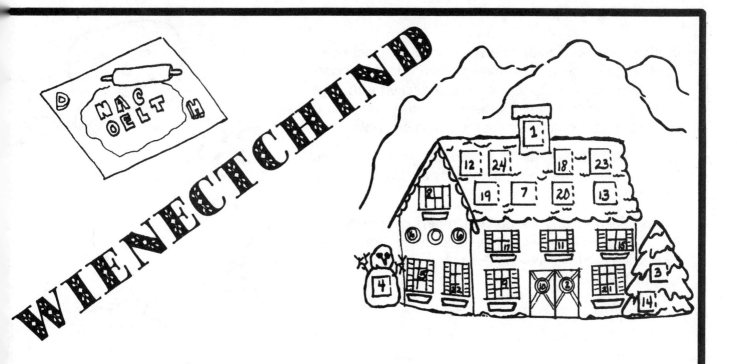

WIENECTCHIND

The Christmas celebration climaxes on December 24. In the village of Hallwil, *Wienectchind* (Christmas Child) walks through the town wearing a white robe and carrying a lantern. Six girls wearing rose-colored dresses accompany her. They visit families, sing carols together and give cakes and cookies to children.

Switzerland's four languages are intermixed with the Christmas spirit. Merry Christmas greetings are recognized in many ways.

Weinhnachten—German
Noel—French
Natale—Italian
Nadel—Romansh

Advent calendars are very popular with children. The numbered windows are opened each day during the Advent season. Calendars can be purchased but are most often made in schools.

Prepare a batch of sugar cookie dough. Trace the letters that spell the four Christmas greetings. Use them as patterns for letter cookies. Poke holes in the tops of the letters and bake until a light brown. When cooled, string a red ribbon through the letters and wear them as a necklace or place them on your tree for a garland.

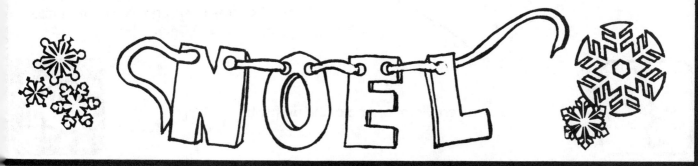

GA1326

In the city of Zurich, *Sechseläuten* is celebrated. *Sechseläuten* means "six ringing bells." On the second or third Monday in April, Zurich is bedecked with flags. Its people celebrate the fourteenth century rebellion of the local craft workers against the rich merchants.

In the 1800's the guilds controlled the government, but in recent years the twenty-five guilds became exclusive men's clubs.

During *Sechseläuten* the guild members parade through the streets wearing elaborate costumes. Some wear historical costumes looking like military uniforms of the Colonial period.

SECHSELÄUTEN

As the parade winds down to 6:00 p.m., the marchers proceed to the town square. There the *Böögg*, or bogeyman, is burned. The Böögg looks like a big snowman. It is made of cotton, filled with explosives, and sitting on a huge pile of wood. Singing, dancing and bands playing continue while the Böögg burns. It is said that the sooner the Böögg burns, the sooner spring will come!

Children have a parade of their own. They wear either historical costumes or imaginative ones.

Each guild has its own emblem and dress according to the trade it represents. The guild of tailors has a big scissors and during the parade, marchers cut off scarves and ties of the spectators. The boatmen carry baskets of fresh fish and throw them into the crowds as they march by.

Design an emblem for one of the twenty-five guilds.

Fastnacht Carnival

The largest and most popular festival in Switzerland is the Fastnacht Carnival. In Basel, ten to twenty thousand masked participants celebrate the three days before the beginning of Lent.

A theme for the parade is chosen months ahead, and it is depicted in costumes, masks, lantern scenes and leaflets. These contain prose and verse about the theme.

The festivities begin at 4:00 a.m., in the market square. Men dressed in bright costumes and wearing huge, strange masks poke fun at the local government. Fife and drum bands and other costumed marchers swing lanterns as they parade through the streets. They try to make as much noise as possible. The masks and noise are said to drive out the cold of winter, and the clanging bells ring in the spring!

In the evening the parade begins again. Masked musicians and marchers carrying lanterns create a spectacle. Often the parade and partying goes on until 4:00 a.m.

Decide on a theme. Make a folded leaflet containing a story, a poem and a costume depicting that theme.

GA1326

SWITZERLAND

ZIPPIN' ON...

Find Out About. . .
- Knabenschiessen in Zurich. Boy's marksmanship is important in Switzerland.

- Alpine Pageant in June that features cow fights

- May Day traditions in Begnins

- Carnival Rice, a custom in Ticino

- Achetringele in Laupen on New Year's Eve

VALUABLE RESOURCES

Bailey, D., and E. Cooper. *Switzerland—Starters Places*. London, England: Macdonald Educational Limited, 1985.

Inglefield, E. *Flags*. New York: Prentice-Hall Press, 1987.

Lands and Peoples Encyclopedia. Danbury, CT: Grolier, 1987.

Schrepfer, M. *Switzerland—The Summit of Europe*. Minneapolis: Dillon Press, 1989.

Swiss National Tourist Office. *Popular Customs and Festivals in Switzerland*. Washington, D.C.

GA1326

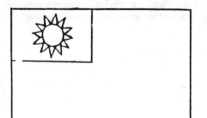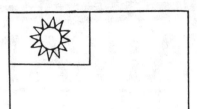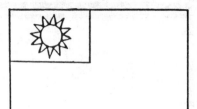

TAIWAN

REPUBLIC OF CHINA

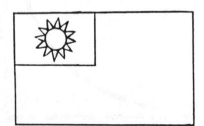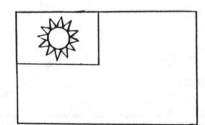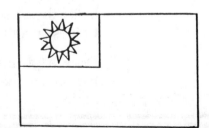

127

TAIWAN

The Republic of China (Taiwan) was founded in 1912. The capital city of Taipei was founded in 1957. Taiwan is a large island located about 110 miles (176.99 km) southeast of mainland China. The flag shows a white sun in a blue sky over a crimson ground. It represents the spirit of increasing progress.

REPUBLIC OF CHINA

1. Taipei*
2. Chilung
3. Tainan
4. Taitung
5. Kaohsiung
6. Hualien
7. Taichung

The plum blossom is the national flower. It has delicate pink and white colors and a light fragrance. It flourishes in the winter and resists the severe cold. It is said to symbolize the perseverance of the Chinese people.

Draw a picture of the plum blossom in the circle.

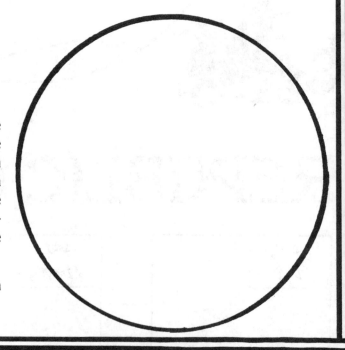

128

GA1326

Lantern Festival

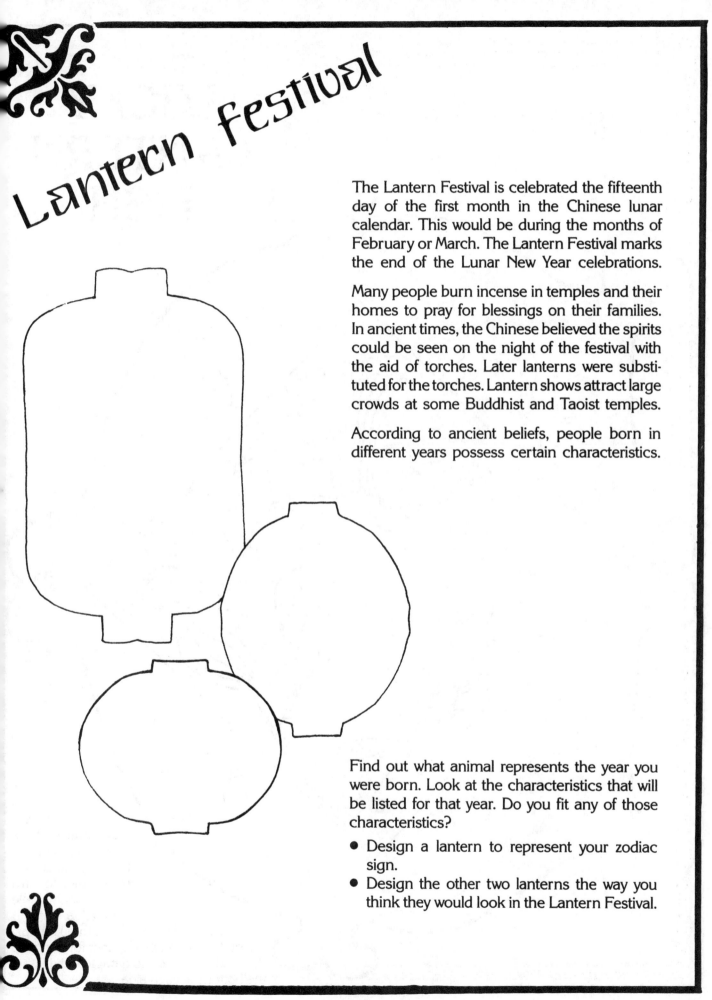

The Lantern Festival is celebrated the fifteenth day of the first month in the Chinese lunar calendar. This would be during the months of February or March. The Lantern Festival marks the end of the Lunar New Year celebrations.

Many people burn incense in temples and their homes to pray for blessings on their families. In ancient times, the Chinese believed the spirits could be seen on the night of the festival with the aid of torches. Later lanterns were substituted for the torches. Lantern shows attract large crowds at some Buddhist and Taoist temples.

According to ancient beliefs, people born in different years possess certain characteristics.

Find out what animal represents the year you were born. Look at the characteristics that will be listed for that year. Do you fit any of those characteristics?

- Design a lantern to represent your zodiac sign.
- Design the other two lanterns the way you think they would look in the Lantern Festival.

GA1326

A lantern with a fish on it is a lucky symbol. Use this pattern to make a lantern.

LUCKY LANTERN FISH

Staple

Punch

Punch

Staple

Color and cut out three of these lanterns. Glue onto heavy paper. Staple three corners to form a triangle. Punch a hole at the top. Attach a string to each side. Gather the three strings, knot them and use the knot for hanging. Add glitter or gold paint and a tassel at the bottom of each side.

130

GA1326

Dragon Boat Festival

The Dragon Boat Festival (also known as the Double Fifth Festival) occurs on the fifth day of the fifth moon of the lunar calendar. This is usually in June. The Dragon Boat Festival is one of the three most important festivals in Taiwan.

According to legend, a famous Chinese scholar named Chu Yuan came into disfavor with the king. At 37 years of age, Chu Yuan tied some stones to his chest and jumped into the Milo River in the Hunan Province. The common people respected Chu Yuan and jumped into the river to try to rescue him. The Dragon Boat Festival commemorates their unsuccessful attempt.

In Taiwan today the main event of the festival is the racing of 42-foot (12.74 m) dragon boats. A helmsman, drummer, twenty-two oarsmen and flag catcher are one crew. Two boats race against each other at one time. There are teams of women and foreigners, also. The ornate heads and tails of the dragons are attached to the boats only for the races. A ceremony takes place before the race when incense and firecrackers are lit to bring the dragons to life. Taoist priests paint the eyes, put paper money in the mouths and throw water on the dragons to rid them of evil spirits.

In the homes, cleaning is important. Medicines and herbs are added to the foods to prevent diseases and promote good health. Sachets of spices and medicines are fastened to the clothing of children. Children try to collect as many of these sachets as possible. Older people get them from their families to show respect for a long life. One of the special foods eaten during this festival is rice dumplings called *tzungtzu*.

- Find a recipe and make rice dumplings for everyone to sample. Learn how to fold them before they are cooked.

- Make soap carvings of the dragon boats. Hold your own races.

- Make life-sized boats on mural paper. Add a life-sized crew. Display in your hallway.

GA1326

MATERIALS
thin material such as nylon netting
potpourri or spices
thread (doubled), embroidery floss, yarn or ribbon
needle
tassel

1

Cut two circles 2"
(5.08 cm) larger
than the desired
finished size.

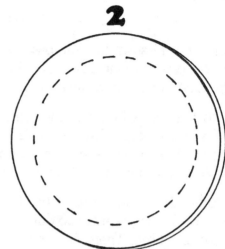

Cut 2.

2

Pin or glue
the two
pieces to-
gether 1"
(2.54 cm)
from the
edge.

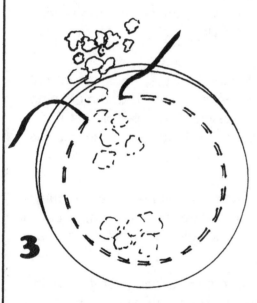

LONG
LIFE
SACHET

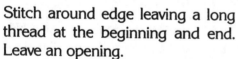

3

Stitch around edge leaving a long
thread at the beginning and end.
Leave an opening.

Stuff the circle pocket with potpourri
or spices.

4

Finish stitching. Pull long
threads gently to gather and
ruffle the sachet.

Tie a bow with the thread or
add a bow of ribbon or yarn.
Make a tassel and add to the
bottom.

5

*The sachet material could
be decorated before stitching, if desired.

GA1326

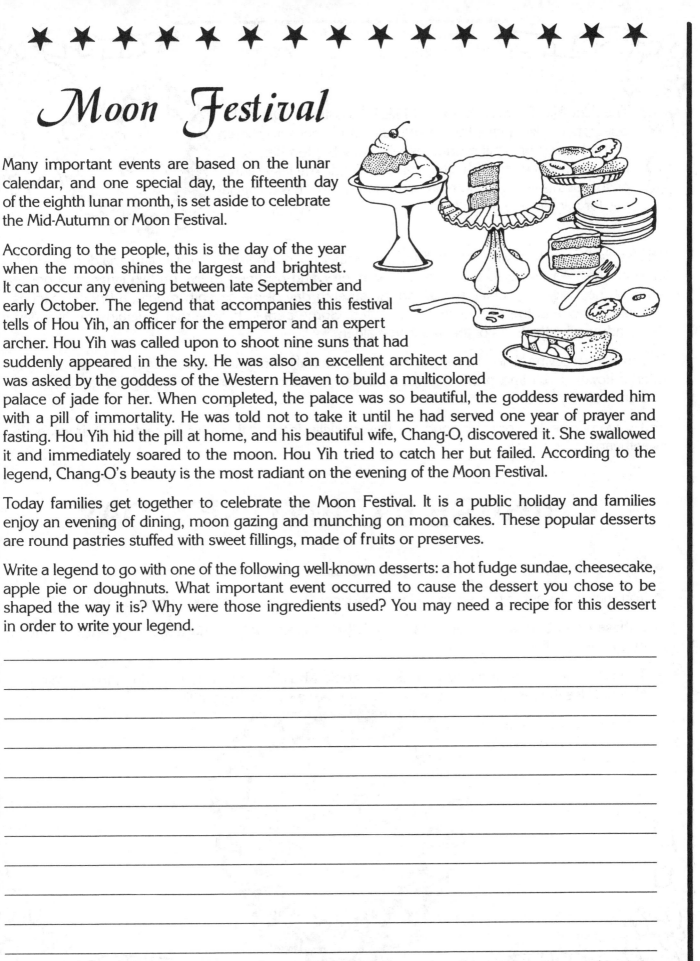

Moon Festival

Many important events are based on the lunar calendar, and one special day, the fifteenth day of the eighth lunar month, is set aside to celebrate the Mid-Autumn or Moon Festival.

According to the people, this is the day of the year when the moon shines the largest and brightest. It can occur any evening between late September and early October. The legend that accompanies this festival tells of Hou Yih, an officer for the emperor and an expert archer. Hou Yih was called upon to shoot nine suns that had suddenly appeared in the sky. He was also an excellent architect and was asked by the goddess of the Western Heaven to build a multicolored palace of jade for her. When completed, the palace was so beautiful, the goddess rewarded him with a pill of immortality. He was told not to take it until he had served one year of prayer and fasting. Hou Yih hid the pill at home, and his beautiful wife, Chang-O, discovered it. She swallowed it and immediately soared to the moon. Hou Yih tried to catch her but failed. According to the legend, Chang-O's beauty is the most radiant on the evening of the Moon Festival.

Today families get together to celebrate the Moon Festival. It is a public holiday and families enjoy an evening of dining, moon gazing and munching on moon cakes. These popular desserts are round pastries stuffed with sweet fillings, made of fruits or preserves.

Write a legend to go with one of the following well-known desserts: a hot fudge sundae, cheesecake, apple pie or doughnuts. What important event occurred to cause the dessert you chose to be shaped the way it is? Why were those ingredients used? You may need a recipe for this dessert in order to write your legend.

_____

_____

_____

_____

_____

_____

_____

_____

_____

_____

_____

GA1326

The Chi Hsi Festival is the Chinese Valentine's Day. This celebration takes place the seventh day of the seventh month of the lunar year. This month, usually early September, is the time when legendary "ghosts" roam the land. The festival that occurs at this time has nothing to do with ghosts! It is a special day for people who are in love.

The story that is told with this holiday remembers a cowherder and weaving maiden who fell in love. They were separated by the Jade Emperor and destined to live on two stars at opposite sides of the Milky Way. Once a year, on the seventh day of the seventh month, a bridge reaches across the sky and the two lovers are reunited. Some people believe that if it rains on this day, the raindrops are the tears of the Weaving Maiden.

Because the Weaving Maiden is said to possess wonderful needlework skills, the girls have traditionally offered flowers, fruit and prayers to the goddess. In return the girls are hoping for good sewing and embroidery skills.

Today, women seldom pray for good needlework skills. Instead, they give presents to their valentine sweethearts.

CHINESE VALENTINE'S DAY

- Try your needlework skills by making an embroidered valentine.

- You may also want to try making a fancy paper cut valentine. Use red or pink paper.

- If these do not show off your skills, bake heart-shaped cookies and decorate them with tubes of colored frosting.

- The valentine card on the next page is for people who did not pray hard enough to the Weaving Maiden! Use the pattern to make a card for someone special in your life.

GA1326

Below is a valentine card you may want to
give to someone special on the Chi Hsi
Festival Day.

MATERIALS
6" (15.24 cm) doily, colored paper for heart, your picture, colored markers, crayons, stickers, conversation heart candy

Cut out the heart below using colored paper. Fold the small window
and cut to open. Position and glue picture on doily so that picture
shows through the window. Glue heart onto doily.

Write this message on the heart:

Open the Window and You Will Find,
Someone Who Wants You for a Valentine.

CUT
CUT
FOLD

OPEN THE
WINDOW...

BE   MINE

135

TAIWAN

ZIPPIN' ON...

- Learn about the goddess Kuan Yin. She is depicted with 1000 hands and eyes.

- Fishermen celebrate the birthday of the Goddess of the Sea, Matsu. What is the legend?

- What do pagodas represent?

- Find out more about the "Ghost Month."

- Research the life and sayings of Confucius.

- Aboriginal tribes in Taiwan also hold festivals. Read more about them.

VALUABLE RESOURCES

Ministry of Communications. *Festivals and Folk Arts, Taiwan*. Taipei, Taiwan. C.T. & T. Communications, 1989.

Official Guidebook, Taiwan. Tourism Bureau of Taiwan, 1989.

Republic of China. Taipei, Taiwan: Kwang Hwa Publishing Company, 1987.

Tourism Bureau of Taiwan. New York.

TURKEY

GA1326

TURKEY

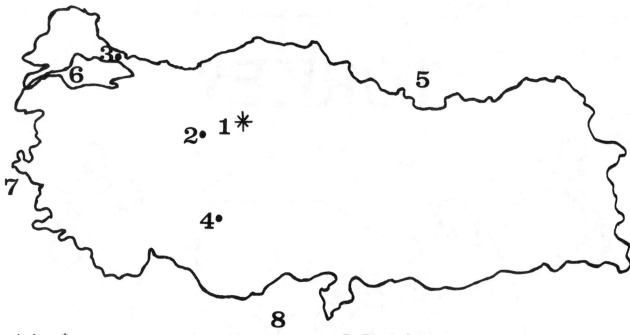

1. Ankara*
2. Yassahoyuk (Gordion)
3. Istanbul
4. Konya

5. Black Sea
6. Sea of Marmara
7. Aegean Sea
8. Mediterranean Sea

Turkey is a country that is located in both Europe and Asia. It has 4968 miles (8000 km) of beaches on four different seas.

It has a long history and lavish culture, rich foods and an interesting future.

The red flag bears the crescent moon and five-pointed star in white. One legend that is told about the flag symbol is that the army of King Philip of Macedon tried to capture Byzantium (now Istanbul). They dug under the city walls at night. The crescent moon was so bright that the soldiers were discovered and the city remained safe. The crescent moon became the symbol of the city.

The star may be the morning star mentioned in the Koran or the symbol of Christianity.

GA1326

Mevlana Ceremony

The city of Konya is one of the oldest cities in Turkey. It was one of the greatest cultural centers during Roman times. During the twelfth century, the Moslem mystic Mevlana Celaleddin Rumi founded the sect of the Whirling Dervishes. The former seminary is now a museum containing the writings of Mevlana.

Every year during the first half of December there is a Commemoration of the Whirling Dervishes. A traditional whirling dance is performed symbolizing the shedding of earthly ties.

When you hear the name *Whirling Dervish*, what do you picture?

How could this picture be tied to a religious teaching?

Use your imagination and list the ten rules you think all Whirling Dervishes should follow.

Every sect had its own uniform or attire. Draw a sketch of what you think a typical Whirling Dervish would look like.

Now, try to find more information about this Moslem sect. How do your ideas compare with the actual sect's teachings?

**Official Whirling
Dervish Attire**

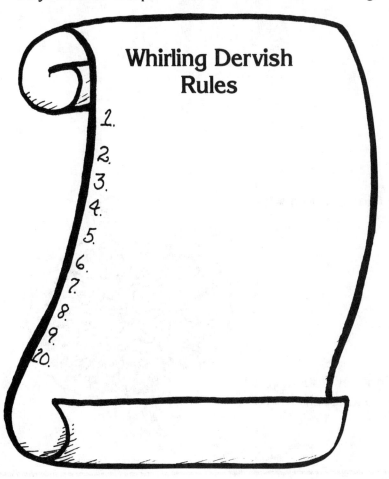

**Whirling Dervish
Rules**

1.
2.
3.
4.
5.
6.
7.
8.
9.
10.

GA1326

The Legends of Gordion

Several legends are associated with early rulers. The city of Gordion is said to be the site where several legends took place. Alexander the Great, it is told, cut the Gordion Knot that gave him the key to Asia.

The well-known King Midas is also entombed in Gordion. Refresh your memory of King Midas' Golden Touch by reading this famous story.

Try to find out more about Alexander the Great. What was the significance to the cutting of the Gordion Knot?

Write a letter...

After reading the "Golden Touch" of King Midas, write a letter to the daughter pretending you are the king.

Write a legend...

Write a legend of your own. Instead of a "golden" touch, you have the chocolate touch, pasta touch, diamond touch or wild animal touch. Use your imagination!

GA1326

TURKEY

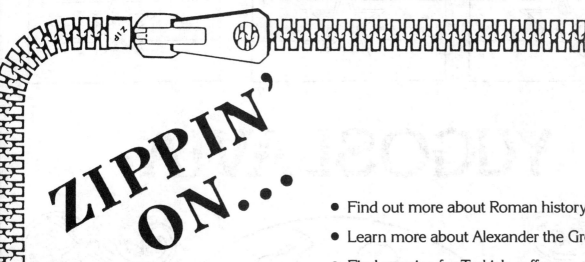

ZIPPIN' ON...

- Find out more about Roman history.
- Learn more about Alexander the Great.
- Find a recipe for Turkish coffee.
- Turkey is known for its rugs. Design a rug using some of the traditional designs.
- Try to find a sample of the famous confectionary, Turkish Delight.

VALUABLE RESOURCES

Ministry of Culture and Tourism. Turkish Tourism and Information Office. New York. 1989.

Pitman, P. M. *Turkey: A Country Study.* Library of Congress, Federal Research Division, 1988.

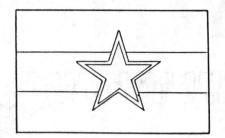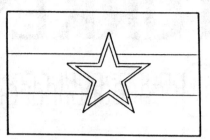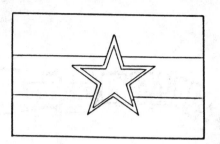

YUGOSLAVIA

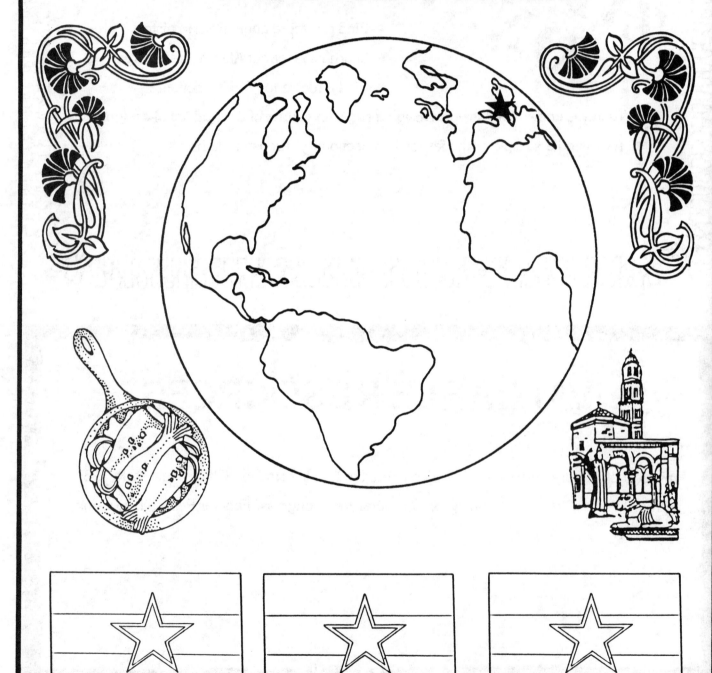

142

YUGOSLAVIA

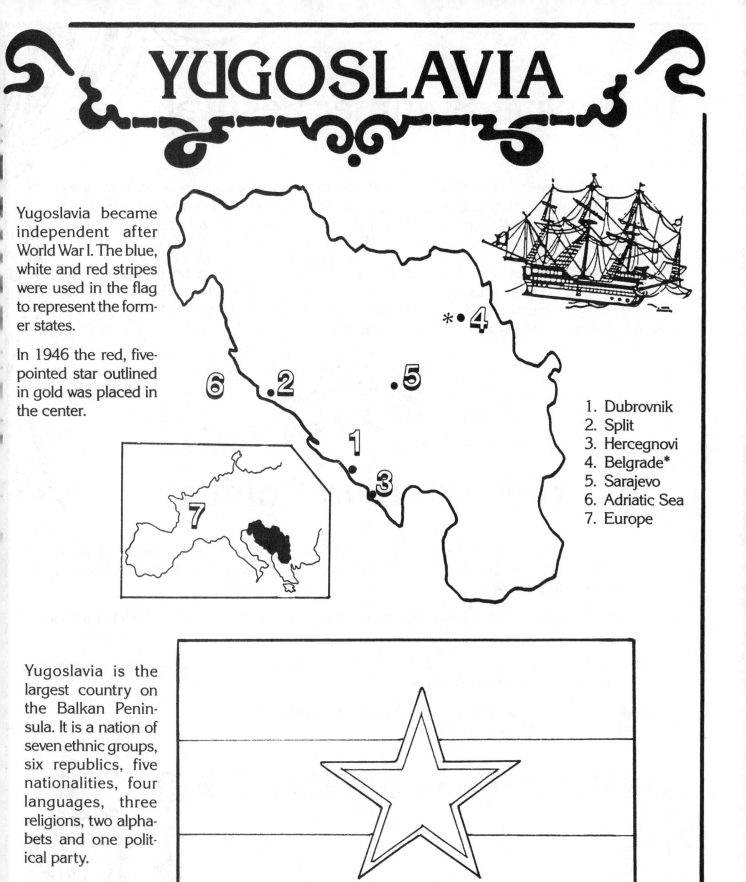

Yugoslavia became independent after World War I. The blue, white and red stripes were used in the flag to represent the former states.

In 1946 the red, five-pointed star outlined in gold was placed in the center.

1. Dubrovnik
2. Split
3. Hercegnovi
4. Belgrade*
5. Sarajevo
6. Adriatic Sea
7. Europe

Yugoslavia is the largest country on the Balkan Peninsula. It is a nation of seven ethnic groups, six republics, five nationalities, four languages, three religions, two alphabets and one political party.

Dubrovnik Summer Festival

The Dubrovnik Summer Festival is the oldest and most popular celebration in Yugoslavia. During the months of July and August, Dubrovnik becomes an international spectacle. Shakespeare's *Hamlet* is performed in an open-air theater. Yugoslavs and foreign performing artists make the famous play come to life.

Read the play *Hamlet* or an interpreted version of it. Who are the main characters? Try putting on this famous play using the language of today. What could be the modern day setting, problems, solutions and ending? Work in groups and try to do the final production in about five to ten minutes without props or scenery.

Sinj Iron Ring Contest

The Sinj Iron Ring Contest takes place during the Split Summer Festival. This tournament for horsemen takes place in August. The most popular contest during the festival is between the horse-mounted lance throwers.

Besides the many horsemanship contests, the Summer Festival also has opera, ballet and concert performances.

How do you picture the horse-mounted lance throwers and the iron ring beginning a contest? What are the rules? What determines a winner?

Below, draw a picture of what you think this contest would look like.

Split

GA1326

Yugoslavian Cuisine

Yugoslavia is located on the shore of the Adriatic Sea. The coastal cities are proud of their fine seafood cuisine. National festivals to intimate family gatherings include ethnic specialties.

The following is a recipe prepared in the ancient walled city of Dubrovnik. It serves four to six people.

Dalmatian Fish Stew

½ c. (125 ml) cooking oil
2 onions, sliced
2½ lbs. (1.125 kg) fish fillets (cut into bite size)
6 tomatoes, peeled, seeded and chopped

salt and pepper
2 T. (30 ml) vinegar
½ c. (125 ml) dry white wine (optional)
chopped parsley

1. Sauté onion in hot oil, add fish and brown lightly.
2. Add tomatoes, salt, pepper, vinegar and wine.
3. Simmer in open pan on low heat for one hour.
4. Serve with parsley accompanied with cooked rice.

Mimosa Holiday

The Mimosa Holiday is a flower spectacle held during the months of January and February. The park in Hercegnovi has over one hundred kinds of tropical and subtropical plants. This flower festival is widely known and admired.

The city of Hercegnovi is located at the entrance to the Bay of Boka Kotorska and is a renowned summer and winter resort area.

What kinds of plants would be found in this spectacular flower display? _____

_____

Check your answers by researching tropical and subtropical plants.

With this research, make a travel poster for the city of Hercegnovi. Advertise the Mimosa Holiday.

GA1326

YUGOSLAVIA

ZIPPIN' ON...

- Learn more about the Folklore Festival in Zagreb.

- Learn about the traditions of the Grape Harvest Celebration in Serbia.

- Look for and try more native recipes including Turkish coffee.

- Predict the future for the country of Yugoslavia and Communism.

VALUABLE RESOURCES

Young, M.S. *Cities of the World* (Vol. 3). Detroit: Gale Research Company, 1982.

Yugoslav National Tourist Office. New York.

Worldmark Encyclopedia of the Nations (Vol. 5). New York: Worldmark Press, Ltd., 1988.

GA1326

CHRISTMAS

Around the World

Date:

Time:

Place:

"Merry Christmas" in Many Languages

Merry Christmas is spoken in many languages around the world. Below is a list of countries and their special holiday greetings. Circle each country in the word search below.

Belgium—Zalig Kerstfeest
China—Sheng Tan Kuai Loh
Denmark—Glaedelig Jul
England—Happy Christmas
Finland—Hauskaa Joulua
France—Joyeux Nöel
Germany—Froehliche Weihnachten
Greece—Eftihismena Christougenna
Ireland—Nodlaig mhaith chugnat
Italy—Buon Natale

Mexico—Feliz Navidad
Netherlands—Hartelijke Kerstroeten
Norway—Gledelig Jul
Poland—Boze Narodzenie
Portugal—Boas Festas
Romania—Sarbatori vesele
Spain—Felices Pascuas
Sweden—God Jul
U.S.S.R.—Hristos Razdajetsja
Wales—Nadolig Llawen

```
P O R T U G A L Y D N A L O P Z
C H I N A F N A D B K E C G Y A
B R C O E Q U E C S J I X B H L
R D K R A M N E D B X I T K B S
T N W W O V C A X E H T Z A E Y
Z A F A J M S W M T W E L K L L
I L E Y D I A G R G K S X R G Y
M G E D X L H N E T S F D Z I N
W N O D E X T M I L R I N I U A
U E X S U H M I C A H A A M M M
S D N A L R E H T E N I L N N R
S E C E E R G R T Z M Y E Y X E
R F I N L A N D E C N A R F W G
A B R X W U S P A I N I I E R X
```

GA1326

Christmas "Santas"

Research more about these Christmas gift bearers. Write a few sentences about how they deliver presents, what they put the gifts in, when they appear, etc. Try to find a picture or imagine what they look like. Draw pictures of as many different "Santas" as you can. Use these pictures on your banners or as ornaments on the international Christmas tree.

Austria:	Christkind	Germany:	Kriss Kringle, Christ-
Belgium and	Nöel		kind or St. Nicholas
Netherlands:	St. Nicholas, Christ-	Italy:	Befana
	kind and Black Pete	Japan:	Santa Claus
Brazil:	Papa Noel	Mexico:	Three Kings
Denmark:	Julnisse	Poland:	Star Man or
England:	Father Christmas		Wise Men
Finland:	Old Man Christmas	Spain:	Three Kings
France:	Pére Noel or le Petit	U.S.S.R.:	Babouschka

An International Christmas Tree

Use the suggested ornaments to decorate an international Christmas tree. There are many patterns available for these ornaments, or provide a variety of materials and have each group create an original ornament design for a special country.

Australia:	cookies in the shapes of koalas, kangaroos, etc.
Brazil:	parrots, chocolate Kisses
Germany:	stockings, candy canes
Great Britain:	royal crowns, bells
Israel:	dreidl, menorah
Italy:	candles, crèche
Kenya:	African masks, feathers
Mexico:	God's eyes, poinsettias
Nigeria:	fish and netting
Spain:	matador, hand fans
Sweden:	straw goats, flags on a string
Switzerland:	cross-country skis, St. Bernard dogs
Taiwan:	hand fans, flowers
Turkey:	stars, flags
U.S.S.R.:	Matryoshka dolls
Yugoslavia:	flowers, flags

GA1326

Christmas Banners

Enlarge one of these patterns for a banner. On the banner display the name of the country, flag, Christmas "Santa," Christmas greeting, anything unique about the country. Or on separate banners, display all the ways to say *Merry Christmas*, all the different "Santas," all the different flags or a globe with as many flags as possible.

151

Make a Christmas house out of a refrigerator box. Cut it open. Bend the two end flaps back to help it stand. Cut out the windows and doors, add window frames, shutter pictures, etc. Attach Christmas twinkle lights around each window and door. Behind each set of shutters attach a scene from a different country. Include the name of the country.

The Christmas house can be used as a bulletin board or the scenery for your Christmas performance.

CHRISTMAS HOUSE

Merry Christmas
to
Everyone
in the
World

152

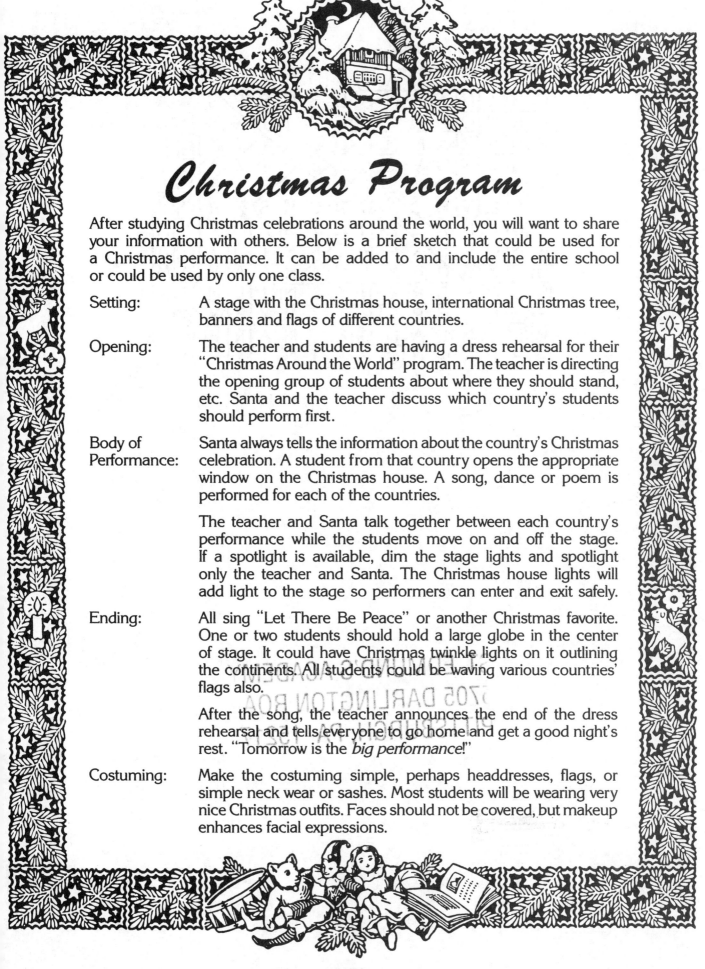

Christmas Program

After studying Christmas celebrations around the world, you will want to share your information with others. Below is a brief sketch that could be used for a Christmas performance. It can be added to and include the entire school or could be used by only one class.

Setting: A stage with the Christmas house, international Christmas tree, banners and flags of different countries.

Opening: The teacher and students are having a dress rehearsal for their "Christmas Around the World" program. The teacher is directing the opening group of students about where they should stand, etc. Santa and the teacher discuss which country's students should perform first.

Body of Performance: Santa always tells the information about the country's Christmas celebration. A student from that country opens the appropriate window on the Christmas house. A song, dance or poem is performed for each of the countries.

The teacher and Santa talk together between each country's performance while the students move on and off the stage. If a spotlight is available, dim the stage lights and spotlight only the teacher and Santa. The Christmas house lights will add light to the stage so performers can enter and exit safely.

Ending: All sing "Let There Be Peace" or another Christmas favorite. One or two students should hold a large globe in the center of stage. It could have Christmas twinkle lights on it outlining the continents. All students could be waving various countries' flags also.

After the song, the teacher announces the end of the dress rehearsal and tells everyone to go home and get a good night's rest. "Tomorrow is the *big performance!*"

Costuming: Make the costuming simple, perhaps headdresses, flags, or simple neck wear or sashes. Most students will be wearing very nice Christmas outfits. Faces should not be covered, but makeup enhances facial expressions.

GA1326

Answers to page 148:

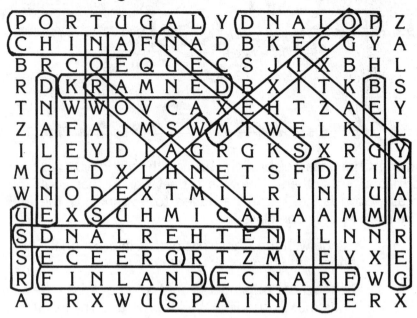

ST. EDMUND'S ACADEMY
5705 DARLINGTON ROAD
PITTSBURGH, PA 15217